PRIMARY TEACHER
50 TEACHING INTERVIEW QUESTIONS & SUGGESTED RESPONSES

Mark Thomas
Lynne Ryder

Disclaimer

The following work endeavours to provide a quality service to help aspiring teachers to gain employment in a difficult and competitive job market. We do not guarantee a teaching position, either full or part time; nor do we guarantee that applicants and participants will gain a job interview. The authors are not responsible for anyone failing their interview as a result of the information contained within this guide. In addition, we cannot guarantee that any course, review of application service, or our on-line training materials will assure a job interview, interview success or employment in teaching.

Every effort has been made to ensure that the information contained within this guide is accurate at the time of publication. However, the authors cannot accept any responsibility for any errors or omissions within this guide.

INTRODUCTION :

THE SUCCESSFUL INTERVIEW

Few events in life are as traumatic as attending an interview or at least that is what received wisdom tells us. This seemingly universal fear has given rise to countless self-help books on 'overcoming interview fears', 'dispelling those interview nerves', and so on. In many respects, this over emphasis on the terror dimensions of interviews is somewhat misguided. Fundamentally, an interview is a conversation between yourself and a small group of adults who are willing you to do well. They are usually friendly, yet formal in tone.

Of course, gaining a teaching job is not a breeze. There is a lot of competition, with far more prospective employees than there are posts. It is a sobering thought that if you are actually invited to attend an interview, the odds of your ultimate success have instantly risen from approximately 1:80 (at the initial application stage) to 1:6 (by the interview stage). With the gravity of such statistics, it would obviously be profligate not to thoroughly prepare for this final part of the process.

It is perhaps important at this stage to state that interviews are not solely dependent on some seemingly mechanical ability to answer a set of questions. It is much more subtle and complex than that. Yes, your preparation on answering possible interview questions is extremely important. However, employers are also looking for a wide range of skills and attributes such an ability to teach, effective communication, someone who is warm, enthusiastic, conscientious, a good team player, reliable, and so on. There is also an element of luck in the whole process.

Other dimensions also come into play: your ability to introduce yourself, a create a favourable impression; personal appearance; your mastery of nerves, body language etc. These areas are covered in detail on our website. Each is important in subtle and sometimes subconscious ways.

Preliminary Preparation

- To some degree, certain types of interview questions can be predicted. Before the interview, you need to practise your own response to these key questions and we would suggest that you embark upon a 'mock interview' either informally, with friends; or as a participant in more formal coaching workshops. Many candidates even use electronic devices to record themselves answering prospective questions. Whichever approach you favour, articulate your anticipated responses – it is amazing how practising the fluidity of your answer dramatically improves the quality of your presentation.

- Almost invariably, application packs contain a person specification and job description for a particular post. You need to be familiar with both. It is a fair bet that some of the interview questions will come from these specifications. Take the time to mentally evidence each area to best 'showcase' your individual strengths and achievements. Make your answers personal to your own context. Maximise your experiences without being fallacious.

- Be familiar with the school. Before interview: review the school's website, online prospectus, most recent OFSTED report, SAT results, awards gained etc. Websites such as goodschoolguide.co.uk offer useful information on prospective schools.

One question which seems to be becoming more prevalent is: 'From our website, what do you consider to be the greatest strengths of our school?' If you haven't visited the site, don't attempt to bluff the answer!

- Be aware of contemporary educational issues appearing in the news (eg Times Educational Supplement). Don't be afraid to occasionally use your knowledge in the actual interview: 'On the theme of reading, there was an extremely good article in the TES which discussed OFSTED's focus on....'

  In addition, the areas of focus in OFSTED inspections can (occasionally) be referred to: 'It's really interesting that the new inspection schedule focuses so much on SMSC ....'
  Try to ensure that such references appear natural and erudite, rather than contrived and inappropriate.

- Before the interview, visit the school – be aware of your transport arrangements, where to park (ensure that you have change for a parking machine), how long the journey will take, whether there are any congestion charges etc. Take an earlier bus, or train to be absolutely sure that you will arrive in plenty of time. In case of unforeseen pitfalls, make sure that you have the school's phone number available. Don't be late.

- Your appearance matters. Ensure that your attire is prepared well in advance. I have known two candidates arrive late for an interview as they were buying shoes (not together).

How to Present Yourself in an Interview.
- Arrive early. Be friendly and cordial with all staff you meet – it is amazing how many members of staff pass comment to the Head Teacher on the demeanour of

applicants. Be aware that in this world of global surveillance, the waiting area may be watched on camera. Also, turn your phone off.

- It very much matters how you enter the interview room. Knock before entering. From the outset smile and stand upright. Make eye contact with the panel and introduce yourself: "Hello I'm Mark (if your name is Mark), it's nice to meet you." Maintain eye contact with each member of the panel as you shake their hand (Give a firm handshake – it is a frequent criticism of candidates that they 'had a flimsy handshake'). Finally, when invited, sit down in the interview chair.

- Your communication, both verbal and non-verbal is extremely important. It is, after-all, the stock in trade of a teacher. Sit upright, with your feet on the floor (rather than sitting 'cross legged'). Cup your hands on your lap to avoid fidgeting. When responding to a question, make eye-contact with each member of the panel.

- Be positive and enthusiastic. Avoid any negative criticism of another school.

- Don't be afraid to ask for a question repeated. Equally, if you are utterly stumped by a question, you can request further clarification. However, try to avoid doing this more than once.

- Your dress code really matters. Research cited by the BBC (What do the colours you wear say about you?) suggests that 55% of the impact you make at work depends on how you look and behave - only 7% on what you actually say. A statistic perhaps open to debate, yet undoubtedly, dress code says a lot about a person.

According to research done by John T Molloy ('Dress for Success'), the most effective interview attire is a dark suit, with a white shirt for men, or white blouse for women; ties should be a dark colour; shoes, a plain brown, or black. These colours, or so research claims, denote a person who is authoritative, reliable, intelligent and trustworthy. Psychologists even go as far as to say that subtle reflections of the school's colours (eg. wearing a green tie to reflect the green of the school uniform etc.) indicates a candidate that has a good 'corporate philosophy' – someone who will fit in to school. Although this seems a little farfetched, it is undeniable that our perception of personality operates at a subtle and subconscious level.

There certainly seems to be sartorial elements which are best avoided, this bracket includes cartoon ties, socks which resemble Jackson Pollock paintings, visible thongs which extend up the back like a badly fitting parachute, chunky rings on each finger etc.

- At the end of the interview, you will (usually) be asked if you have any questions. The majority of candidates decline with the response: "No, I think we have covered everything…" This is a wasted opportunity as a well intentioned question can reveal a lot about a candidate. For a moment, put yourself in the panel's shoes and consider these questions from a candidate:

    I see from your website that you offer a wide-range of extra-curricular activities, as I'm a qualified gymnastic coach, would I have an opportunity to lead an after school gym club?
    When I visited school, Mr West mentioned the 'Young Carers' initiative, I was wondering how this is progressing?

- Both questions suggest a positive psychology, someone who is eager to be involved in the corporate life of school and someone who is enthusiastic and caring. If the panel's decision is not 'clear cut', a prudent question could well be the deciding factor.

- Just as first impressions matter, so does the final impression that you create. At the end of the interview, shake each member of the panel's hand and thank them. At this stage, a final (brief) statement can be really powerful:

    "I would like to thank you for inviting me along to interview today. I've actually really enjoyed the experience and if I were successful then I promise you that I will work extremely hard and bring a lot to the life of the school."

Interview Questions and Suggested Responses.

It is almost impossible to predict every interview question that you will be asked. However, there are certain types of questions which frequently make their way into the interview arena. There tends to be certain categories of questions: the warm up (eg. Tell us a little about yourself...); the motivational question (What skills would you bring to this role?) and the situational/task question (Can you give us an example of how you have dealt with a disruptive pupil?). Make your responses precise, try not to waffle. With situational questions, try to follow the STAR sequence: what was the **situation** or **task**? What **actions** did you take to improve/tackle it? What was the (successful) **result**? The following questions are broadly organised into different themes. These are: the ice breaker; general motivational questions, class and wider school based scenarios; pedagogic questions, specific questions relating to a key stage or a school denomination; finally, concluding questions.

INTERVIEW QUESTIONS AND SUGGESTED RESPONSES

1. Tell us about yourself

Initial Considerations:

This is a question generally designed to put you at your ease, but nonetheless one that you need to give careful consideration to. A clear, concise well-rehearsed answer (of no longer than 2 minutes) will not only relax your own nerves but will give the interviewers the impression that you are confident and articulate. The interviewers are really more interested in what sort of person you are rather than in your home life and circumstances (although you may want to include some limited information about this). It is a real opportunity to sell yourself so ensure that you include all the interesting facts about yourself- for example have you completed the Duke of Edinburgh Award or are you a member of one of the Cadet Forces? Details such as these give a real insight in to the person you are.

Suggested Response:

It is difficult to give you a tailored response to this question as it will obviously be very personal to you. Some key adjectives to describe yourself might be : motivated; enthusiastic; dedicated; organised; team player; positive.

- *'I am the youngest of three children and currently still living at home with my parents. My parents and family are very important to me and they have always encouraged and supported me in following my ambition to become a teacher.*
- *I would describe myself as someone who is motivated and enthusiastic – especially if I have a particular goal in mind. For example when I was asked as Junior Officer in the Air Cadets to organise a weekend activity for the younger cadets I was commended by the Commanding Officer for my enthusiasm and motivation in organising the event.*
- *I am also have a very positive person, which I feel is extremely important, especially when working with children. Friends tell me that I am a good person to be around because of my 'upbeat' nature and positive outlook on life'.*

2. Tell us about your teaching experience to date

Initial Considerations:

Again, this may be an opening question designed to put you at your ease, but like question one, a well considered and rehearsed answer will make you appear confident and articulate. Ensure that your answer demonstrates the breadth of experience you have had, whilst also taking the opportunity to highlight your skills and abilities.

Suggested Response:

Again it is difficult to give you a tailored response to this question as it will obviously be very personal to you.

- *'The teaching experience I have gained during my degree course has been very varied and has offered me the opportunity to work in both Key Stage 1 and 2.*
- *During my first block practice I worked in a Y1 class in an area of high deprivation. There was a high percentage of children on the SEN register, which meant that I had to clearly differentiate for these pupils, giving due regard to their IEPs. I was also fortunate enough to observe how the class teacher reviewed IEP s with parents and given the opportunity to make a contribution to this process.*
- *My second placement was in a Y5 class. I was responsible for 80% of the teaching during this practice and I achieved grade 1 s for all of my observations; which I was particularly*

pleased about as there were a few pupils with challenging behaviour in the class. However, this did give me the opportunity to develop a number of positive behaviour strategies.

- *During all my practices I have also taken every opportunity to broaden my experience. I attended all staff meetings, which was particularly useful in terms of my own development and I helped to run after school activities including a drama club and a healthy eating club'.*

3. What attracted you to this post?

Initial Considerations:

This question is often asked by interviewers and is designed to test how enthusiastic you are about the job. It also gives you an opportunity to show how much research you have done about the school. Your response should not include reference to the attractive salary or convenience of the location – even if this is part of the attraction!

Suggested Response:

- *'I know from my research that this is a good school, where the pupils are encouraged to be independent learners and achieve well. I would relish the opportunity to be part of such a successful school. Having read the person specification and job description I believe that I have the right skills and abilities to make a valuable contribution as a member of staff.*

- *I was also particularly interested to read about your links with the school in Austria. I studied German to A level standard and would love the opportunity to teach German in the classroom'.*

4. What are your greatest strengths?

Initial Considerations:

This question gives you a real opportunity for you to sell yourself (without sounding too boastful) and convince the panel that you are the person for the job. You will have read the person specification and job description. They may have points in these documents, for example, the need to be flexible, positive, a 'team player', or have a sense of humour- so ensure that your answer also reflects the sort of person the panel is looking for.

Suggested Response:

- *'I believe that one of my greatest strengths is the fact that I am highly organised as a person. What ever I am doing I like to feel that I am well prepared and organised. I feel that this is particularly important in my role as a teacher as lack of organisation in terms of lesson planning or delivery can have a very negative effect on the children's learning. I was commended during all my teaching practices for my high levels of organisation and preparation.*

- *I consider myself to be very flexible as a person. Having worked in schools, I understand the need to be able to change plans or respond to a situation, with perhaps very little notice. I know that I am able to do this successfully, with very little fuss, I also believe that, as I have taught in both Key Stage 1 and Key Stage 2, I am flexible in terms of which year group I would be able to teach in.*
- *I am also a very positive person with a positive outlook on life. I can usually mange to see a positive aspect to most situations. I believe that being positive as a person influences other people to have a more positive outlook on other people – especially the children'.*

5. We watched you teach a lesson earlier this week: Can you evaluate the lesson for us?

Initial Considerations:

The vast majority of schools will want to observe you teach as part of the interview process. Having observed you teach, it is highly probable that one of the questions in the interview will be asking you to reflect on the lesson. Be prepared and have an informed answer ready. This will show the panel that you are a 'reflective practitioner'. When observing a lesson the observer will usually consider your lesson in terms of:-

- Pace
- Outcomes
- Behaviour and engagement of the pupils

Try to keep this in mind when evaluating your lesson. Even if you feel that the lesson went really well, think about ways in which the lesson could be improved.

Suggested Response:

Your response to this will obviously be based on the lesson and how it went. Remember to be honest – even if you don't feel it went well.

- *'I generally felt that the lesson went very well. I was pleased with the way in which the children responded to me and to the activities I had planned for them. I felt that I maintained a good pace throughout the lesson, which meant that the children remained engaged.*

- *I do feel that the learning objective was achieved by the most of the pupils. However, although I spoke to the class teacher before planning the lesson, I am not sure that I pitched the activity for the more able pupils at the right level. I feel that they were capable of much more and if planning a subsequent lesson I would obviously take this in to account'.*

6. Which curriculum subject would you most like to support/lead?

Initial Considerations:

As a primary school teacher you may be asked to help manage a curriculum subject; or you may be asked to be part of a curriculum team. Although teachers would not be expected to coordinate a subject until they have completed their NQT year, employers are often keen to know what your curriculum strengths are. Being able to offer a strength in an area of the curriculum that the school has little expertise in will be a seen as a positive attribute on your part. Primary schools often lack teachers with expertise in music or modern foreign languages. If you have these skills, make sure that you highlight them at the interview.

Suggested Response:

- *'As I have a degree in History I obviously feel that I would be suited to coordinating this subject. I am passionate about the teaching of history and am very keen to help children to develop their historical enquiry skills. Being curriculum coordinator for history would obviously give me an opportunity to do this.*

- *I also have a great interest in music and love to play the guitar so would also feel confident to take a lead in this subject too.*

- *However, as a primary school teacher I am aware that I may be called upon to coordinate any curriculum subject and would obviously do so to the best of my ability. I would do this by ensuring that I developed my skills in that area as well as possible, through CPD, and by staying up to date with any curriculum developments'.*

7. What do you see yourself doing in five years' time?

Initial Considerations:

This question is often asked to establish what your long term intentions are in relation to remaining at the school. The panel will also want know that they are appointing someone who has some drive and ambition and wants to progress as a teacher. It is often a difficult question to answer, as you do not want to give the impression that you do not intend to remain in the post for very long; nor that you lack ambition; or worse still that you are overly arrogant about your abilities.

Suggested Response:
- *'If appointed to this position, I would obviously expect to be well established within the school and as such to be making a positive contribution to the school's success, by ensuring that my pupils achieve well.*
- *I do consider myself to be an ambitious person and I would hope that during that time I would have taken every opportunity to progress my knowledge and skills as a teacher - either through CPD, or through taking opportunities to be involved in curriculum development. In this way, when the opportunity arises, I would have made sure that I am ready to take the next step in my career'.*

8. What do you consider to be your greatest developmental need?

Initial Considerations:

This is a frequently asked question and one that needs careful consideration. You do not want to jeopardise your chances of success by highlighting a weakness that the panel would view as detrimental. Give careful consideration to the person specification and job description when answering this question. It would not, for example, be wise to say that you need to improve your ICT skills if the person specification identifies excellent ICT skills as an essential requirement. When answering this question it is perhaps best to consider your answer in terms of 'an area for development' rather than a weakness.

Suggested Response:

Many candidates avoid major areas for development (eg. 'I need to improve my behaviour management...') focusing instead on a lesser area which adds 'icing on the cake' – for example, " *I really enjoy the teaching of R.E. but feel that I now need to develop my assessment techniques across all areas of attainment*".

Avoid corny self aggrandisement such as "*I work much too hard....*" etc.

9. Why should we appoint you to this position?

Initial Considerations:

This question provides an opportunity to sell yourself and convince the panel that you really are the person for the job. When answering this question you should think carefully about the sort of person they are looking for (which will be outlined in the person specification and job description).

Suggested Response

- *'Having read the job description and person specification, I believe I have all the necessary qualities you are looking for in a teacher. I am passionate about teaching and know that I have the ability to be an outstanding teacher, which was indicated in the grades I received during teaching practices. If appointed I can assure you that I would be dedicated, hardworking and willing to do whatever it takes to ensure that the pupils in my care achieve their potential'.*

- If the person specification has indicated that certain skills, such as music or modern foreign languages are desirable, you may want to highlight your ability in these areas.

- You may also want to indicate your willingness to run out of school activities (but be careful that you can deliver on promises such as these).

10. We need someone who works well as part of a team. How do you meet this criteria?

Initial Considerations:

If you are asked this question then it is obviously an essential requirement of the job. Ensure you respond positively, highlighting the opportunities you have had to work as part of a team and the qualities that you brought to it.

Suggested Response:

- *'I believe that I am a good team player as I enjoy working collaboratively with others and have found it to be very beneficial. I have had a number of opportunities to work as a part of a team including planning with a colleague from a parallel class, whilst on my teaching practice. This meant that I had to be willing to contribute ideas as well as be open to the ideas of others. In terms of completing tasks allocated to me, I had to be flexible and mindful of my responsibility towards other team members. Feedback from my planning colleague about my contribution was very positive and highlighted my ability to work well as part of a team'.*

11. As a teacher you need to be flexible: How do you meet this criteria?

Initial Considerations:

Again, as with the previous question, if you are asked this question then it is obviously an essential requirement of the job. Ensure you respond positively giving practical examples of when you have demonstrated your ability and willingness to be flexible.

Suggested Response

- *'My experience of teaching in primary schools has highlighted the need to be flexible, especially when working alongside other colleagues, and I believe that I am. On two or three occasions during my last teaching practice I had to make changes to my timetable and plans to accommodate school events or the needs of other staff. This had to be done at very short notice on one occasion, but I showed that I was flexible enough to respond to the situation and adapt my plans for the morning without a fuss.*
- *I also understand the need to be flexible in terms of the hours I work and accept that there will be times when I am required to be available outside of the normal school day. For example, in one school, I helped out with the performing arts club and stayed behind on several evenings to help with this'.*

12. What do you like about our school?

Initial Considerations:

25

This question is designed to find out how well informed you are about the school. It also gives an opportunity for you to ingratiate yourself with the senior leaders of the school, but be careful not to be overly obsequious. Think carefully about how you would answer this question and be careful what you say.

Suggested Response:

- *'Having both researched and visited the school, there are a number of things that I have found that I really like about it. Firstly, I am very impressed by the warm welcome I have received from both staff and pupils – everybody has taken time to speak to me. The high standard of behaviour and excellent manners of the pupils is also something which has impressed me.*
- *I also know from my research that you are an inclusive school, which has high expectations of its pupils – both of which are qualities that are important to me as a teacher'.*

13. What is your own educational philosophy?

Initial Considerations:

It is surprising how similar answers to this question frequently are. Be honest in your response - sincerity (in contrast to well rehearsed rhetoric) tends to show through. Unless you are Aristotle, the more succinct your philosophy, the greater the impact it will have. The following is an example of a typical response:

Suggested Response:

'I believe that all children, regardless of ability, or any other factor, should be treated equally and encouraged to maximize their potential. I firmly believe that education should be inclusive of all, enjoyable, exciting and memorable'.

14. Describe your own teaching style?

Initial Considerations:

Your response needs to demonstrate your flexibility. You also need to be aware that different lessons may demand different teaching styles. You may need to give an example to support your response.

Suggested Response:

- *'I like to ensure that, where possible, my lessons are practical, interactive and skills based. I also endeavour to*

- *plan a range of challenging differentiated are child-centred and progressive.*
- *My actual teaching style varies depending of the activity. For example, in a recent art lesson we explored North American needle work patterns. With a small group, I demonstrated how to form the patterns. This introduction necessitated me modelling a skill. However, with the majority of lessons, I try to make them interactive, for example by breaking up my introduction with a variety of activities in which the children can actively participate – this reinforces the learning and allows them to sustain their concentration.*
- *Problem solving activities, and challenges which demand a range of thinking skills also appear prominently in my lessons'.*

15. How good are you at time management?

Initial Considerations:

To a large degree, interview panels are looking for a member of staff who demonstrates that they are aware of the need for prudent time management in a profession which demands dedication and successful task completion.

Suggested Response:

'I always endeavour to realistically plan my lessons to complete all activities. I realise that lesson timings can be difficult to fulfil if, unrealistically, too much is planned. When evaluating my lessons, I have been self-reflective on my time management and this has helped me to better match my lesson plan to the time available.

- *I also realise that teaching is a profession which demands a high degree of organisation and hard work. With this in mind, I plan a sequence of lessons, and prepare resources well in advance. I also mark the children's work on the day of completion. Meeting deadlines is extremely important to me and I always prioritise tasks and methodically work through them.*
- *Above all, I am fully aware that effective teaching involves the effective use of time. I am prepared to give whatever time is needed to become the best teacher I am able to be'.*

16. Can you tell us about a time when you have had to work under pressure?

Initial Considerations:

At times, we all work under pressure – this may be due to imminent deadlines, the volume of work, or the challenge of completing a set task. The panel are looking to employ a member of staff who can 'handle' pressure through pro-active planning, fortitude, independence, hard work and by maintaining a sense of perspective.

Suggested Response

Responses to this question are very much dependent on your own experiences. Consider the STAR model in response to this question (see introduction).

An example:

> 'Recently, at very short notice, I was asked if I would abandon my plans for my afternoon lessons in order to lead a video-conferencing session with our partnership school in Germany. This was not a huge problem as I could rearrange my plans. However, I realised that there were certain logistical issues – such as activating the video link- which I needed to quickly overcome. After a lot of perseverance I was finally able to do this - with the help of our IT co-ordinator. The outcome was well worthwhile – the pupils had a fantastic opportunity to speak to their partners and to practise their German. It was really quite a memorable afternoon!'

This response reveals a lot about the candidate: firstly, the response follows a logical (STAR) sequence; it also indicates several positive characteristics such as flexibility, dependability, practicality, positivity and an ability to work under pressure!

17. Which part of the job description do you least like?

Initial Considerations

Job descriptions tend to contain a mixture of 'essential' elements (eg. an ability to manage pupil behaviour) and 'desirable' elements (eg. a knowledge of ICT software used in Key Stage 2). There tends to be a certain convention when answering this question : firstly, only select one area of the job description – if possible make it a 'desirable' area. Many people use a potential 'weakness' implied in the question to their advantage. Consider the two responses below:

Suggested Response:

'In the job description, 'a thorough knowledge of the SEN Code of Practice' is detailed as a 'desirable' element. Although I have a good knowledge of the stages, protocols and practices within the present guidelines, I am aware that changes on a national level are imminent. I feel that I need to fully appraise myself of the new proposals and how they will affect me as a class teacher.'

Or:

'In terms of the 'desirable' criteria regarding 'a thorough knowledge of assessment procedures', I feel that although I have a good overview of assessment principles and practices, I would like to develop my ability to assess levels of attainment in different aspects of ICT - I am aware that this can be a particularly difficult area to assess '.

Both responses reveal a genuine need for development yet, at the same time, the areas are very specific and imply an existing depth of knowledge in key areas.

18. Tell us about a recent project or lesson with which you were pleased.

Initial Considerations:

This is quite a common question and tends to focus on the positive outcomes of an activity. Some candidates focus on a singular pupil activity (eg. a swimming lesson in which a child gained her first award) ; others describe a more multi-faceted approach (eg. a cross-curricular project about 'Our Community').

Suggested Response:

The example below follows the STAR sequence:

'Recently we were asked to help restore the ornamental gardens of a local park. This allowed us a fabulous opportunity to work with different groups including landscape designers. The children planted their own produce and looked after their own 'veg - patch'. Watching the seeds grow was awe-inspiring and the children felt really proud of their work; they also developed lots of skills such as perseverance, co-operation and patience. One little boy, who was very reluctant to talk, constantly asked the gardeners questions about the different seeds, he really 'came out of his shell' – the project was worthwhile for this one incident!

In the autumn, we were able to harvest the vegetables and we invited a local chef into school to help us develop some special recipes. I imagine that many of the children will remember the project for years to come…'

19. How would you establish your class rules?

Initial Considerations

All schools and classrooms need rules in order to function effectively and safely. Most classrooms will have these clearly displayed – look out for them on your tour of the school. Your response should indicate how you would involve the pupils in establishing class rules.

Suggested Response:

- *'As a new teacher, establishing classroom rules would be a priority when starting to work with any new class.*
- *I would ensure that the pupils were involved in the process by allowing them to work in small groups to come up with suggestions for class based rules. This would be followed with an opportunity to share ideas before agreeing as a whole class what the rules should be. In this way pupils would feel that they had ownership of the rules and they would be more meaningful to them'.*

20. Can you describe what your ideal classroom would look like?

Initial Considerations:

The response to this question will obviously depend on the age group of the children. A Year 6 classroom will obviously look very different to a Reception classroom. However, there are certain elements that all good classrooms should have (for example all resources should be clearly labelled and easily accessible).

Suggested Response:

When answering this question give careful consideration to the year group the post is advertised for. For example, if it is for a reception class ensure you mention 'continuous provision areas' and outdoor play.

You should include the following points in your response:-

- Displays would be bright and informative and include examples of children's work from a range of subjects.
- Resources would be well organised, clearly labelled and accessible to all pupils.
- Seating and tables would be arranged to allow flexibility in terms of grouping of children. This may include a carpet area for younger children.

Your answer may also include reference to :-

- Role play areas
- Book or library corners
- Working walls
- Interactive displays
- ICT
- Writing areas
- Continuous provision or structured play.

21. How would you deal with a disruptive pupil?

Initial Considerations:

A frequently asked question. The phrasing of the question may be: 'How would you deal with a pupil who is reluctant to engage in a lesson?' The question also has links with question number 22.

The panel, understandably, need to be convinced that they are employing someone who is mature, non-aggressive and strategic in their response. You need to be self-assured that you possess these attributes.

Suggested Response:

- *'Before starting any new role, I would appraise myself of the school's 'Discipline' or 'Pastoral Management Policy' in order to familiarise myself with the school's reward systems, and the established consequences for unacceptable behaviour.*

- *As a class teacher, I would consult with key staff to familiarise myself not only with the academic attributes of pupils, but also their pastoral needs. Understandably, I would ensure through differentiation that pupils can fully engage in enjoyable lessons, with lots of positive reinforcement.*

- *After taking these preliminary steps, if a pupil is disruptive I would endeavour to deal with the situation in an objective, non-confrontational and strategic way - with a minimum of fuss. Depending on the situation, and if it were necessary, I would ensure that any consequences are effectively pursued and I would appraise my line manager of the situation'.*

22. What would you do if a child threw an object across the classroom?

Initial Considerations:

All interview panels will be interested to know how you will approach issues of behaviour and discipline. They will often present you with a scenario such as this one. This is also linked closely to question 23.

Suggested Response:
- *'With any new class one of the first things I establish are class rules and expectations, as well as rewards and consequences (these would obviously be in line with the whole school policy). In my previous school, I used a traffic light system to deal with behavior issues – which was extremely effective. I would use these as the starting point for any behaviour issues.*

- *In the instance of a child throwing an object across the classroom, I would speak to the child about the incident to establish why it had happened, reminding them of the class rules and consequences. I would move the child from where they were sitting, closer to me or another adult. I would also ensure that the child faced a consequence - appropriate to the misdemeanor (eg five minutes loss)- in line with the school policy.*
- *If this was not an isolated incident, but rather a repeated pattern of behaviour from the child, I would speak to the child's parents about it and consider putting an Individual Behaviour Plan (IBP) in place'.*

23. Without breaking any confidentiality, can you tell us about the most challenging pupil you have taught and the strategies that you used to deal with the situation?

Initial Considerations:

When answering this question be mindful not to break any confidentiality or appear critical of the child, parent or school, to which you are referring.

Suggested Response:

You will no doubt have experienced a number of challenging pupils during your teaching experience. Choose a child or situation that clearly shows that you are capable of using effective strategies to deal with challenging behaviour.

- When answering this question apply the STAR approach – mentioned earlier.
- Give a brief overview of the situation, in this case the challenging behaviour that the child presented.
- Outline the actions and strategies that you put in to place to address the behaviour issues.
- Highlight the response of the child to the strategies you employed. Ensure that these emphasise the positive impact of your intervention.

24. How do you plan your lessons?

Initial Considerations:

The rationale under-pinning this question is to gauge whether the candidate understands the key components of an effective lesson. It is the type of question in which it is easy to go 'overboard' with too many small details. Keep to the main planning sequence.

Suggested Response:
- *'Where I am able, I like to make my lessons interactive, practical and creative.*

- *I begin by revisiting elements from the previous lesson. As part of my introduction I 'connect the learning' by reviewing previous outcomes and by offering a brief overview of what will be covered in the next lesson.*
- *At an early stage, I clearly identify the appropriate objectives for the lesson. I then examine the success criteria – namely, what the children will need to do to ensure that their learning is good. These are incorporated into a carefully structured introduction.*
- *I ensure that I plan well differentiated activities which are challenging and commensurate with the ability levels of individuals.*
- *I then plan for other key elements such as the resources I will use, key questions, the incorporation of assessment for learning techniques, homework and an effective plenary'.*

25. How do you ensure that you cater for the needs of all pupils in your class?

Initial Considerations:

Obviously this question is designed to find out how you would deal with the range of pupils' abilities you may be faced with. It would not, however, be enough to simply refer to SEN and Gifted and Talented pupils, although these pupils do need to be referred to. Interviewers will also want to know how you differentiate for all pupils, and how you would identify when a pupil may need some intervention to help move their learning forward.

Suggested Response:

- *'As a class teacher I would ensure that I had a clear overview of the range of abilities within the class, including pupils on the SEN and Gifted and Talented registers. I would ensure that the work I provided was clearly differentiated to cater for all groups of pupils – taking in to account IEPs and any particular gifts, abilities and talents.*
- *I would also ensure that I was mindful of pupils' learning styles and any gender bias (eg do I have a group of boys who are reluctant writers?)*
- *Appropriate differentiation of work is paramount to providing for all pupils' needs and abilities, but it is 'ongoing formative assessment' that is key to ensuring that work is appropriately differentiated. I would*

therefore ensure that my daily marking and assessments of the pupils' work clearly informs the work I plan and how it is differentiated'.

At any of these points it would be helpful to give a practical example of how you have put this in to practice.

26. How do you ensure that you include elements of 'Spiritual, Moral, Social and Cultural' Education (SMSC) in your lessons?

Initial Considerations:

Over the next few years, as it has become a key element in the latest OFSTED framework, SMSC will assume a high profile in the majority of schools. To some degree, planning for SMSC will take place at a policy level; however, there will be an expectation on class teachers to plan for realistic opportunities to develop SMSC.

Suggested Response:
- Firstly, I am aware that many schools have a very robust curriculum for SMSC and teach 'SEAL' lessons.
- On a cross-curricular basis, there are certain subjects such as R.E., Geography and History which offer a wealth of opportunities to develop aspects of SMSC. At

the planning stage, these opportunities need to be maximized.

This is very much the type of question which would be enhanced by a brief example from your recent experience. For example:

- *'We recently studied the life of Florence Nightingale as part of a History topic. I realised that the study had fantastic opportunities to explore key elements of SMSC such as 'concern for others' and 'the will to do what is right' (both of which are within the National Curriculum). So I planned for a series of activities looking at 'modern nurses' : we invited a paramedic into school….*

27.What would you do if a child was not handing in their homework?

Initial Considerations:.

Schools will have a homework policy, which can usually be found on the school website. They will also have a 'home school agreement', which usually outlines the expectations of both pupils and parents with regard to homework. Try to make sure that you read these documents before the interview. Your answer also needs to show an awareness that incomplete homework may be a sign of other issues at home, such as parents work commitments or a change in circumstances.

Suggested Response:
- *'When dealing with this issue I would obviously pay due regard to the school's homework policy.*
- *I would speak to the child to find out the reason for homework not being completed.*
- *If the barrier to homework were a home-related issue I would speak to the child's parent to see if the issue could be resolved. I would also stress the importance of homework and offer additional support if necessary.*
- *If the child was struggling with the homework set I would offer additional support, perhaps through attendance at the school's homework club (if the school has one)'.*

28. You will have a Learning Support Assistant (LSA) working alongside you in the classroom. How will you ensure that you use this additional adult support effectively?

Initial Considerations:

It is true to say that these days, most primary school teachers will have some additional adult support in the classroom. This support may be full time, or part time; or an LSA may be there specifically to support a child with additional needs. Whatever the circumstances, employers will want to know that you can plan for, and utilise, this additional resource effectively. It is of note that Ofsted Inspectors take in to account how well classroom support is utilised when making an overall lesson judgement; ineffective use of classroom support can bring down the overall grade of a lesson.

Suggested Response:

You will no doubt have had experience of working with LSAs in the classroom. In your answer, you should incorporate any practical examples of how you made this work effectively. An example of a good response:

- *'I believe that if additional classroom support is to be used effectively then the LSA needs to have a clear understanding of their role, the lesson objective and the children's abilities and needs.*

- *I also believe that it is important that the LSA knows that their contribution towards the children's learning is both welcomed and valued.*
- *In order to achieve this, I always ensure that any LSA working alongside me :-*
- *Is aware of which children are on the SEN and Gifted and talented registers and has access to IEPs.*
- *Has access to my planning and is clear about their role. Prior to the start of the lesson, they are aware of the objectives for groups (or individuals) that they are working with.*
- *Has a clearly defined role within the lesson – particularly during the initial input. For example in my last school, the LSA would always have a small group of 'targeted' pupils to support during this time. This would often be children who had been identified as having problems in the previous lesson.*
- *Has time to discuss and evaluate lessons with me, as well as having the opportunity to contribute ideas for subsequent lessons. In one of my previous schools, it was often difficult to find time to speak to the LSA. So, at the end of the lesson, we used a communication book for her to note any comments or concerns. We both found this very useful and effective'.*

29. What would you do if a parent complained that their child was not making enough progress?

Initial Considerations:

As a teacher this is a scenario you may well face, especially if you are working in an area where parents have high aspirations for their children. As well as outlining how you would deal with the problem, it would also be wise to offer assurances that this is not a scenario you envisage happening.

Suggested Response:

- *'As a teacher I have high expectations of all pupils: I also use regular formative assessments (be prepared to say what these are if asked), as well as daily marking to track pupils' progress, which in turn informs my planning and next steps for learning. I would therefore be extremely disappointed to be faced with such a scenario.*
- *I would make an appointment to meet with the parent to review their child's work and progress in detail. Hopefully, this would reassure them that their concerns were unfounded.*
- *If the parent's concerns were proven to be correct, I would ensure that the appropriate support and interventions were put in to place to address the issue. I may also consider writing an IEP for the child - if appropriate. I would arrange*

a time to meet again with the parent to inform them of my actions and to review the child's progress'.

30. How do you assess pupils' progress?

Initial Considerations:

Assessment is a vital part of the teaching cycle and you should be clear about how you would assess the progress of pupils in your class. Assessment can be both 'formative, which is ongoing and helps to build a picture of the pupil's progress – such as daily marking and levelling of pieces of work; and 'summative', which gives a 'snap shot' of a pupils ability at a given moment in time – such as 'end of unit assessments' or end of year tests. Schools will also have their own policy and cycle for assessment.

Suggested Response:

- *'I would obviously ensure that I am following the school's policy for assessment and I would use the previous year's data and results as a benchmark to measure the progress the pupils are making.*
- *I would ensure I used a range of formative assessments such as quality daily marking, including regular leveling of pieces of work, weekly test scores and guided reading and writing sessions. I would also ensure I had a good*

system for recording my assessments, in order to help me build up a picture of the pupil's progress.

- *I would also use summative assessments such as end of unit tests and end of year tests – in line with school policy'.*

31. How would you use data to track pupils' progress?

Initial Considerations:

Pupil progress data is of great importance to the DFE; and an overarching focus for Ofsted Inspectors when making a judgement about how effective a school is. Head Teachers therefore want to know that prospective teachers know how to use data to track pupils' progress.

You should know that pupils are expected to make 3 sub levels progress (eg. from Level 2a to 3a) across two years and therefore at least 1 sub level progress (eg. from level 2c to 2b within a year).

You should also be aware that Key Stage 2 pupils are expected to make 2 levels progress by the end of Year 6 based on their Key Stage 1 results (eg. a child who scored 2c in Reading at the end Key Stage 1 would be expected to achieve Level 4c by the end of Key Stage 2).

Suggested Response:

- *'I would start by using the previous year's results and data to set end of year targets for each child. The targets would be based on the child making 2 sub levels progress across the year – for example a child who achieved 3c at the end of the previous year would be given an end of year target of 3a. I would then use results and data from both formative and summative assessments to monitor the child's progress to see if they were on track to achieve their target. Using data to track progress in this way would mean that I could provide timely interventions and support for those pupils who may be in danger of underachieving.*
- *I would also ensure that targets were shared with both pupils and parents'.*

32. If a child in your class was seriously underachieving, whose fault would you consider it to be?

Initial Considerations:

At the end of the day the responsibility for pupil achievement lies with the class teacher. However, there may be other barriers to learning, such as issues at home or specific learning difficulties.

Suggested Response:

- *'As a class teacher I believe that the responsibility for any underachievement ultimately lies with me. I am passionate about my job and would take it personally if a child was seriously underachieving, rather than looking for excuses. There may of course be external barriers to the child's learning that lie beyond the classroom, such as home circumstances. However, as class teacher I would see it as my responsibility to help the child over come any barriers to learning, which may of course involve liaising with parents and outside agencies'.*

33. How would you incorporate 'Assessment for Learning' (AFL) into your lessons?

Initial Considerations:

Assessment for learning is a powerful way of raising pupils' achievement. It is based on the principle that pupils will improve most if they understand the aim of their learning; where they are in relation to this aim and how they can achieve the aim (or close the gap in their knowledge). It is not an 'add-on' or a project; it is central to effective teaching and learning.

One of the assessment for learning principles states: 'Teachers should equip learners with the desire and the capacity to take charge of their learning through developing the skills of self-assessment'

All successful lessons should include elements of AFL.

<u>Suggested Response:</u>

- *'In order for AFL to be most effective, children need to know what the next steps are in their learning and how they can achieve them. I would therefore ensure that pupils had clear targets for their learning that were referred to at the beginning of lessons. I would also ensure that each lesson objective was supported by clear success criteria, that the children could use to assess their own learning. Throughout the lesson I would include 'mini plenaries' when the learning objective and success criteria were referred back to.*
- *I use a variety of AFL strategies during my lessons, some of these have included: peer marking; marking ladders; traffic light systems; thumbs up and pupil comment sheets. I have found each of these strategies particularly beneficial in terms of focusing the pupils on their learning and helping them to assess for themselves if they have achieved their target or learning objective. I also ensure that pupils' work is quality marked with 'next steps' for learning clearly indicated'.*

34. How can setting targets for pupils help to raise standards?

Initial Considerations:

This question is closely linked to the previous one. If schools are going to raise standards then pupils, as well as teachers, need to know what they are aiming for. Targets set for the pupils need to be meaningful, achievable and regularly reviewed.

Suggested Response:

- *'Target setting for pupils is an effective way of moving their learning forward. Pupils need to know what they need to do in order to improve and clear achievable targets, which are reviewed regularly, help with this process.*
- *For example, during my last teaching practice I set pupils' targets for their writing, which were based on my marking of their work. They noted the targets that I gave to them at the front of their books and referred back to them at the start of each writing lesson. I encouraged the pupils to note at the end of their work whether or not they thought that they had achieved their target. I found that this was a very effective way of focusing the pupils in to their next steps for learning. Because the targets were regularly reviewed and relevant to the pupils writing I found that they had a positive impact in terms of improving the standard of their work'.*

You should also include any examples you have from your own practice that highlights how target setting can help to raise standards.

35. How do you achieve a high standard of work in pupils' books?

Initial Considerations:

In many respects, there are two dimensions to this question: firstly, how you establish a culture of high expectation and secondly, how this is manifest in the children's work.

Suggested Response:
- *'Firstly, there needs to be an ethos of high expectation in the class, where children are challenged to meet their maximum potential.*
- *Within the children's books, there needs to be an expectation that work will be presented neatly, in accordance with any school 'Presentation Policy'. At the start of each term, I would spend time reinforcing my expectations for presentation. I would also ensure that handwriting skills are developed throughout the year.*

- *Regarding the content of work, at the planning stage teachers need to make sure that work is differentiated so that pupils can engage in meaningful and challenging lessons which extend key aspects of the curriculum. Pupils' progress should be furthered by the use of meaningful individual targets, extension work and 'next step' marking which clearly identifies areas for development.*
- *Over a period of time, you would also expect to see some evidence of curriculum enrichment including cross curricular links, the use of ICT and activities which develop 'Spiritual, Moral, Social and Cultural' education'.*

36. What would you consider your role to be in terms of safeguarding?

Initial Considerations:

As part of 'safer recruitment' all employers are obliged to include questions related to safeguarding in the interview process. Every person that works with children has a 'duty of care' towards them: interviewers want to know that you clearly understand your responsibility in this area.

Every school has clear policies and procedures for dealing with safeguarding, which may be included on their website. If possible try to have a look at them before the interview.

Suggested Response:

- *'As a teacher I obviously have a duty of care towards all pupils, which I know extends beyond the classroom. I would therefore make it a priority to apprise myself of the school's policies and procedures in terms of safeguarding; including identifying who the 'named' Teacher and Governor for Safeguarding are (if you have seen the school's policies and procedures make reference to them at this point).*
- *As a teacher I would always be mindful of the pupils' safety and welfare by being vigilant and noting any changes in behaviour or appearance. I would promptly report any concerns I may have in line with the schools policy to the appointed person.*
- *I understand that, should a child disclose something to me, I must never promise to keep it a 'secret', and I would make the child aware of the need to pass the information on to the appropriate people. I also understand that it is not my role to question the child or investigate what has been said, but simply to pass on the information to the appropriate person'.*

37. What would you do if a child disclosed something to you which was a cause for concern?

Initial Considerations:

This is obviously a safeguarding issue and is closely linked to question number 36. You must be mindful of your 'duty of care' to the child when answering this question. It would be helpful to have accessed copies of the school's Child Protection Policies and Procedures   (these can often be found on the school website) prior to your interview.

Suggested Response:

- *'As a class teacher, I am aware that I have a 'duty of care' to all pupils and would therefore take any such disclosure very seriously. As soon as possible, I would ensure that I reported my concern to the 'named person for safeguarding' – whom I note in your school is Mrs X - following the school's policy and procedures. If, however, the disclosure was a 'child protection issue' where I considered that the child was at risk from significant harm or had sustained a visible injury, I would ensure that my concerns were conveyed to the 'named person' immediately. If that person was not immediately available, I would ensure that my concerns were passed to the most senior person in charge'.*

You should also add the following :

- *'I understand that, should a child disclose something to me, I must never promise to keep 'secret' what they have told me; and would make the child aware of the need to pass the information on to the appropriate people. I also understand that it is not my role to question the child or investigate what has been said but simply to pass on the information to the appropriate person'.*

38. What would you do if a parent came to tell you that they thought that their child was being bullied?

Initial Considerations:

Bullying and harassment can take many forms and is an issue which all schools take very seriously. All schools will have clear policies and procedures for dealing with incidents of bullying and harassment. These can often be found on the school's website - it would be helpful for you to read them prior to the interview.

Suggested Response:
- *'I would obviously take any allegations of bullying or harassment very seriously and would make time to speak to the parent about their concerns.*

- *Having spoken to the parent, I would reassure them that their concerns have been taken seriously and make them aware of the need for time to investigate their allegations further. I would also arrange for a time later that day when I could speak with them again about the matter.*
- *I would then ensure that I dealt with, and recorded the incident, in line with the school's policy and procedures, which I have found out in this school are …'* (here you would outline, briefly, the school's own policies and procedures).

If you are not aware of the school's policy you might say the following:-

- *'In my previous school this would have included: speaking to both the victim and perpetrator to establish what exactly had happened; ensuring that the perpetrator faced appropriate consequences in line with school policy; offering support to the victim providing follow up PSHE work with the whole class'.*

39. How would you deal with an angry parent?
<u>Initial Considerations:</u>
Unfortunately, this is a scenario that teachers do find themselves faced with from time to time.

Schools may well have a set of procedures for dealing with such instances, which may include a zero tolerance of aggressive or abusive behaviour from parents – if this is the case notices expressing this will be on display in the reception area of the school. You should always remain polite and calm when dealing with an angry parent. Although you may want to speak to an irate parent away from the earshot of other parents and pupils, you should also be mindful of your own safety – make sure that other members of staff are around to give assistance if needed.

Suggested Response:

- *'When dealing with such a situation, I would obviously be mindful of any school policies or procedures, ensuring that I remained calm and polite through out the conversation.*
- *If approached on the playground, I would ask the parent to move to a less public place, but would ensure that another of member of staff was aware of the situation.*
- *If appropriate, whilst acknowledging their concerns, I would politely point out to the parent that they were being aggressive or shouting and ask them not to do so. Once they had calmed down, I would endeavour to find*

- *out what their concerns were and deal with them appropriately.*
- *If the parent continued to be angry or aggressive, I may well ask them to make an appointment for the following day, hopefully allowing them to calm down and be more reasonable in their approach. After the parent had left, I would make a more senior member of staff, or the Head Teacher, aware of the situation and possibly ask for their support at the next meeting'.*

40. How would you go about developing parental links ?

Initial Considerations:

Parents, carers and families are by far the most important influence in a child's life; their support can play a vital role at all stages of a child's education. In many respects the responsibility for developing parental links in school will lie with the Senior Leaders. However, it is also important that teachers are able to develop effective links with the parents and carers of pupils in their class. Developing effective channels of communication is the key point to emphasise when answering this question.

Suggested Response:

- *'I believe that establishing good parental links is key to children fulfilling their potential. Therefore, as a teacher it is very important that I am able to establish effective means of communication with parents. I notice from looking at letters to parents on your website that you provide an opportunity for parents to meet with class teachers early in the year – this would provide an ideal opportunity to establish a working relationship with them.*

- *When dealing with parents, I always try to ensure that I am friendly and approachable in order to put parents at their ease. It is vital to effective communication that parents feel that they can approach a teacher about a problem.*

- *On going communication with parents about their child's learning is also an effective way to develop parental links. In my previous school, as well as letters home about specific learning events and activities, I used the child's homework diary as a means of communication. Parents were encouraged to comment on their child's homework and I found that this 'two way' communication was a very positive way of developing links with the parents as well as encouraging them to become involved in their child's learning'.*

41. What do you consider to be the qualities of a good teacher?

Initial Considerations

I am sure that you will be well aware of the many qualities needed to be good teacher – ensure that you can articulate what they are if asked a question such as this.

Suggested Response:

- *'A good teacher needs many qualities which include : good subject knowledge; organisational skills; a willingness to be flexible and the ability to plan and deliver creative and effective lessons. These not only motivate pupils, but meet their individual needs. In addition, a really good teacher is dedicated to their job and is willing to do whatever it takes to ensure that pupils achieve all that they are capable of'.*

42. What are the elements of a good lesson?

Initial Considerations:

> There will be many opinions and theories about what constitutes a good lesson; however, when asking this question most panels will have in mind the Ofsted criteria for lesson judgements.

Under the new 2012 Ofsted framework, the key elements that would be looked for in order to judge a lesson as good are: the outcomes for all pupils – ie do all groups of pupils (SEN, G&T, Free school meals pupils etc) make progress in the lesson; the pace of the lesson; the behaviour of the pupils; the use of formative assessments (AFL) and the deployment of support staff.

The Ofsted evaluation schedule for school inspections outlines very clearly what is required for teaching to be judged as good – this can be found on the Ofsted website.

Suggested Response:

A good lesson should have the following elements to it:

- A clear learning objectives, underpinned by clear success criteria that the pupils can use to assess their learning against.
- An exciting short introduction to stimulate enthusiasm, promote thinking and engage the pupils from the start.
- Well-planned, differentiated activities that move all groups of pupils forward in terms of their learning.
- The lesson should be well paced , in order to ensure that all pupils stay engaged – behaviour should be good.

- As well as a plenary at the end, the lesson should also provide opportunities for 'mini plenaries' throughout, in order to to re-engage pupils and focus them back to the learning objective and success criteria.
- Any additional adults should be effectively employed to support the pupils learning.
- Opportunities for pupils to assess their own learning (AFL) should be clearly planned for.

43. What makes an outstanding teacher?

Initial Considerations:

This question is linked to question 41, which outlines the qualities of a good teacher. Outstanding teachers, obviously, have all the qualities of a good teacher but they also have an innate ability to teach creative and inspirational lessons that motivate pupils as well as the passion and drive to ensure that all the pupils achieve highly.

Suggested Response:

- An outstanding teacher possesses all the qualities of a good teacher which include: excellent subject knowledge; organisational skills; a willingness to be flexible; and the ability to plan and deliver creative and

effective lessons, which engage pupils and meet their individual needs. But an outstanding teacher also has an innate ability to enthuse and motivate all their pupils, through their own creativity, passion and drive.
- An outstanding teacher is willing to go above and beyond what is expected of them to ensure all their pupils achieve their full potential.

44. What are the difficulties in teaching a mixed age class ?

Initial Considerations:

Approximately 15%- 20% of schools have some mixed classes. These tend to be selected either on an 'age' or 'ability' basis. Small schools tend to have a greater proportion of mixed groupings. One common approach to answering such a question is by identifying the challenges offered by mixed classes and how you would tackle these.

Suggested Response:
- *'I realise that there are several challenges with mixed classes, not least the difficulties of covering the National Curriculum. The idea of rotating curriculum coverage needs to be carefully timetabled as it could have long term implications regarding the coverage of programmes of study. I realise that*

- *a phrase often used under such circumstances is 'plan up one year, and down the next'.*
- *In lots of ways, mixed groups offer a real opportunity for a teacher to develop their ability to effectively differentiate activities. This in itself can have a positive affect on pupils' learning. Both of these areas obviously have an implication for teacher planning and the assessment of pupils' progress.*
- *Of course, parents may be concerned about their child being in a mixed aged class but I feel that the positives need accentuating – pupils are in an environment where their needs are specifically met; younger pupils can benefit by their exposure to more challenging 'older' work and a lot of schools state that the greater time with one teacher creates a more nurturing and stable learning environment'.*

45. We are a Church school: How would you promote the Christian ethos of the school?

Initial Considerations:

Most Church schools will not necessarily be looking for a 'practicing Christian' ie somebody who attends church regularly (although Catholic Schools may want you to have the Catholic Teachers Certificate).

However, all Church schools will want to know that they are appointing someone who is sympathetic to and can up hold their Christian ethos.

If you are a practicing Christian make sure you mention this in your answer. The Christian ethos of a school will not only be reflected in the close links the school will have with their affiliated church but through the Christian values which underpin the school. The explicit Christian Values may be referred to on the school website and will almost certainly be displayed around the school. Try to ensure that you are familiar with these before your interview.

Suggested Response:
- *'I know from my research that the Christian ethos of your school is underpinned by the values that you encourage the children to develop, for example: forgiveness, compassion, hope, love. I can see that they are an intrinsic part of the way that the school functions in terms of how the pupils and staff behave towards each other and how you teach them. I would therefore endeavour to uphold those values through the way I behave and teach in your school thus providing a good role model for the children.*
- *I also note that you have very strong links with the local church and I would plan to develop these links through the*

RE Curriculum.' (you may want to give a practical example of how you have done this in other posts or teaching practices).

- If you are a practicing Christian you may want to add the following: *'As a practicing Christian and member of St Paul's Church I would relish the opportunity to work in a Church school, as I feel that it is important for the children to know what being a Christian really means. Through my own experiences I feel that I could help them develop their understanding of this'.*

46. What do you consider to be good Foundation Stage practice?

Initial Considerations

Since September 2008, the Early Years Foundation Stage (EYFS) has become a statutory framework for all early years settings, including school nurseries and reception classes. If you are attending an interview for a position working in the Foundation Stage, you must ensure that you are familiar with the EYFS and the four themes and principles that underpin it. www.birthtofive.org.uk is a very informative site for Early Years practitioners.

Suggested Response:

There are number of elements that would be needed in order to constitute good Foundation Stage Practice. Your answer should make reference to the following:-

- Play based learning.
- A curriculum that is relevant to the children and based on first hand experiences.
- Ensuring that 80% of the learning activities are child initiated. Only 20% of the child's learning should be adult led.
- Classroom organisation that encourages independence and allows the children to 'scaffold' their own learning.
- Continuous provision areas based on the six areas of learning.
- Continual access to high quality outdoor learning.
- Observation led assessments.
- Partnership with the child's parents or carers

47. How would you ensure a smooth transition from the Foundation Stage (Reception class) into Y1?
Initial Considerations:.
Transition involves moving from one environment and set of relationships to another. The process of transition may be viewed as one of adaptation.

Studies have shown that the best adaptation takes place when conditions are similar, communication is encouraged and the process of change takes place gradually over time. This is particularly pertinent to young children making a transition from one stage of their learning to another. If you are being interviewed for a position in a Y1 class, this is a question that you are very likely to be asked. As a Y1 teacher you will need to have a clear understanding of the EYFS and you should also be familiar with the document 'Continuing the Learning Journey' which sets out the best practice for securing a smooth transition from the Foundation Stage to Y1.

Suggested Response:

- *'In order for transition to be successful it is important that it is a gradual process. I would therefore take the following steps to ensure a smooth transition.*
- *I would meet with the Foundation Stage teacher to discuss the EYFS profile results and use them a basis for planning lessons and target setting in the first half term.*
- *I would make sure that the children had opportunities both to work with me and visit the Y1 classroom during the Summer Term – hopefully allaying any anxiety the children may have about the transition.*

- *Ideally there would be an opportunity for me to meet with parents to discuss the transition and any concerns they may have.*
- *The document 'Continuing the Learning Journey' highlights the need for the Y1 classroom and practice to closely mirror Foundation Stage classroom and practice. I would therefore ensure that my classroom had continuous provision areas set up to provide the children with opportunities to initiate their own learning – this would include learning in the outdoors'.*

48. How would you ensure a smooth transition from Key stage 1 to Key Stage 2 (from Y2 to Y3)?

Initial Considerations:

This question is obviously linked to the previous one. There are certain considerations that need to be given to the issue of transition, whatever stage of learning the children are at. The answer to both questions are very similar.

Suggested Response:

- *'In order for transition to be successful it is important that it is a gradual process. I would therefore take the following steps to ensure a smooth transition:*
- *I would meet with the Y2 teacher to discuss the end of Key Stage 1 results and use them a basis for planning lessons and target setting in the first half term.*
- *I would make sure that the children had opportunities both to work with me and visit the Y3 classroom during the Summer Term – hopefully allaying any anxiety the children may have about the transition.*
- *There would also ideally be an opportunity for me to meet with parents to discuss the transition and any concerns they may have'.*

49. Would you be interested in taking extracurricular activities?

Initial Considerations:

If the panel has taken the time to ask this question then they are obviously looking for a positive response from you. However, be sure that you are able to fulfil any promises you make in relation to this question.

Suggested Response

- *'I would certainly relish the opportunity to get involved with extra curricular activities. During my teaching practices, I have helped to run a number of after school activities, including drama and a tennis club. I really enjoyed my involvement in these activities as I felt it gave me an opportunity to get to know the pupils outside of the classroom.*

- *I am very interested in performing arts and would love to be involved in this as an extra- curricular activity- I really believe that it helps to build the children's confidence and self -esteem. However, I would be more than happy to help out with extra- curricular activities in any way I could'.*

50. Have you any questions for us?

Initial Considerations:

Most interview panels will usually end an interview with this type of question. Having a well thought out question to put to the panel will give the impression that you are interested and eager to gain the position on offer. On the other hand, a seemingly irrelevant or arrogant question could be detrimental to your chances of success. Be careful what you ask!

Suggested Response:

The following are some questions that you may consider asking the panel :-

- *'I am very keen netball player and would be interested in running an after school netball club. If I am fortunate enough to be appointed - would this be possible?'* (this question could be adapted to any sort of club or activity you are willing to run in the school)
- *'If I am successful in gaining this position, as an NQT, what training and support would be available to me?*
- *'I am aware that you have just introduced a new skill based curriculum in school and am interested to know if it has been successful'.* (This sort of question shows that you are interested in the school and have done your research.)
- *'I have always found having parents working in the classroom to be very beneficial, how involved are parents at this school?'*

Printed in Great Britain
by Amazon

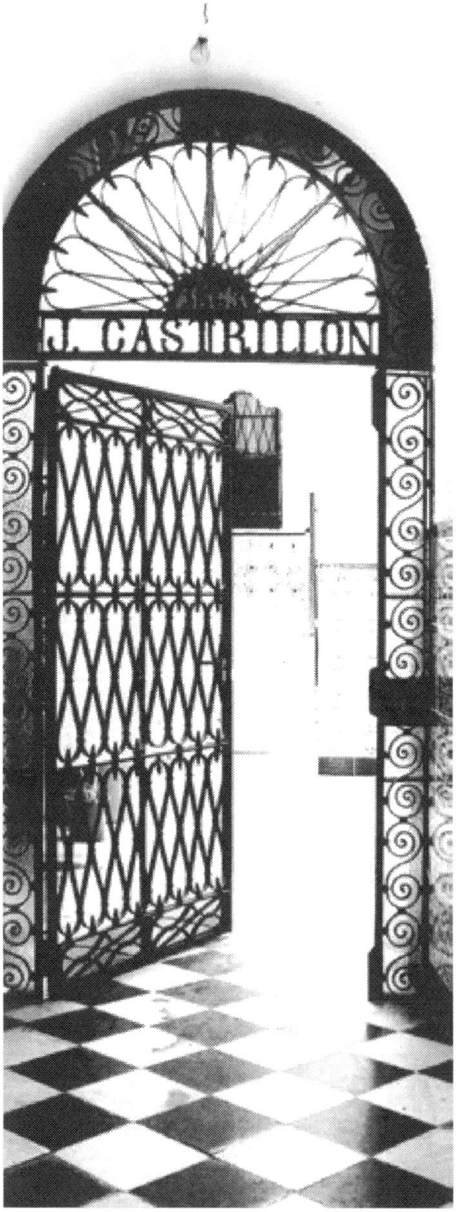
J. CASTRILLON

Dedicated

to the memory of my father

John Edward Rutherford Blundell,

who also loved Spain

and to Alice, who came back

through the looking-glass

and to Marilyn and Brad

Rebecca and Seth

I wish them joy.

Foreword

On my first visit to Vejer ten years ago, as I trundled my case through the town to my hotel, a street name caught my attention; José Castrillón Shelly. Who was this? I wondered; could he be related to our Shelley, the Romantic poet, who died in Italy in 1822? There seemed no way I could find the answer to this, or any of the other questions that came into my mind as I wandered through the streets. When, finally, I became a permanent resident of Vejer, I began researching with a view to finding some of the answers, and writing this book gradually became part of the process. It wasn't until comparatively late, however, that I discovered that the Shelly family arrived from Valencia as the result of one of their sons' marriage to a girl from Vejer, and so probably came to Spain via the British occupation of Minorca between 1708 and 1782. I still have no idea if they were related to the poet; these and other questions are yet to be answered.

One of the most delightful things about Vejer is the pride its people seem to take in their town and its history, though I have also discovered that living in a place so extravagantly historical poses its own problems. Is that piece of broken china you find when you take up the kitchen floor a bit of 1970s junk, or the last remnant of a fifty centuries-old civilization? And if the latter, what then are your chances of getting the kitchen done in time for Christmas?

This book contains very little original research, and in producing it, I have been dependent on the work of Vejeriego historians. The excellent publication 'Boletín', produced by La Sociedad Vejeriega de Amigos del País was an invaluable source, as was 'Janda', an annual publication by the same organization. In this second edition, I have tried to bring a few items up to date, but the original material is basically unchanged.

A bibliography is supplied at the end of the book, but I must stress that any errors are my own. My inspiration and guides were the respected Vejer historians Antonio Morillo and Antonio Muñoz Rodriguez, whose erudite and readable histories of Vejer were invaluable.

I met Señor Muñoz at the launch of another book and took the opportunity to clear up a mystery that had haunted me since I first began to investigate the history of Vejer. Several people have asked me to confirm that there really is a lake beneath the church, complete with boats. Approaching the historian, I was glad to see that he had a twinkle in his eye as I asked this unusual question. And his answer? You'll have to read the book...

Callejón de Amaro, April 2014

Thanks and Acknowledgments

As already mentioned, this book makes use of the work done by an army of Vejeriego archaeologists and historians, and I am happy to take a further opportunity to thank them. I would also like to thank the numerous Vejeriegos I have pestered for information while researching this book. Many are not known to me by name, but I would particularly like to acknowledge the help of Dolores Moreno Servan, José Ortiz, Oscar Olivier Bertrand and Carmen Marchan for patiently answering my questions. Ängel Tinoco Chirino was kind enough to fill in some of the gaps in my information, and I am particularly indebted to the staff of the library in Vejer for their help in finding research material.

Thanks also to the Real Sociedad Económica de Amigos del País de Vejer for permission to reproduce photographs from their publication Memoria de Vejer, and in particular to Antonio Muñoz Rodríguez, Café Chirino, J.M.Basallote, Purificación Pérez, Chamorro Rodríguez and Archivo Casa Mas for permission to reproduce photographs in their possession, and crucially, to Juan Begines for his help in arranging this.

Particular thanks are due to Dr. Brycchan Carey for his guidance on the matter of slavery and Juan José Ruiz López for taking the time to explain Carnaval, as well as Adrián Brenes Ureba for his help with the section on Flamenco. Special thanks must go to Rebecca Cornwall for a brilliant cover design.

I would also like to thank the people who read the first edition and made comments. I have not been able to accomodate them all, but I have responded to one particular suggestion by including some maps.

Above all, I would like to thank the people of Vejer de la Frontera for their love and care for this beautiful town and their kind response to a foreigner; and the town council for their work in preserving Vejer's heritage and history.

CONTENTS

PART ONE: THE HISTORY 9

Chapter 1 Iberia 11
Chapter 2 Tartessos 25
Chapter 3 Turdetania 18
Chapter 4 Hispania Baetica 29
Chapter 5 Vandalucia 35
Chapter 6 Spania 37
Chapter 7 Landa-Hlauts 39
Chapter 8 Al-Andalus 43
Chapter 9 Narguillén 51
Chapter 10 Vegel 77
Chapter 11 Andaluzia 63
Chapter 12 'The Land of Jesus, within two steps of Paradise' 85
Chapter 13 Vejer 101
Chapter 14 Costa de la Luz 118

PART TWO: LEGENDS 123

PART THREE: CUSTOMS AND CULTURE 135

PART FOUR: BUILDINGS, MONUMENTS AND PLACES OF INTEREST
.... 149

PART FIVE: THE STREETS OF VEJER 167

BIBLIOGRAPHY 176

'Bejer de la miel' (Vejer of the honey)
Agustin de Horosco, XVI century

PART ONE

THE HISTORY

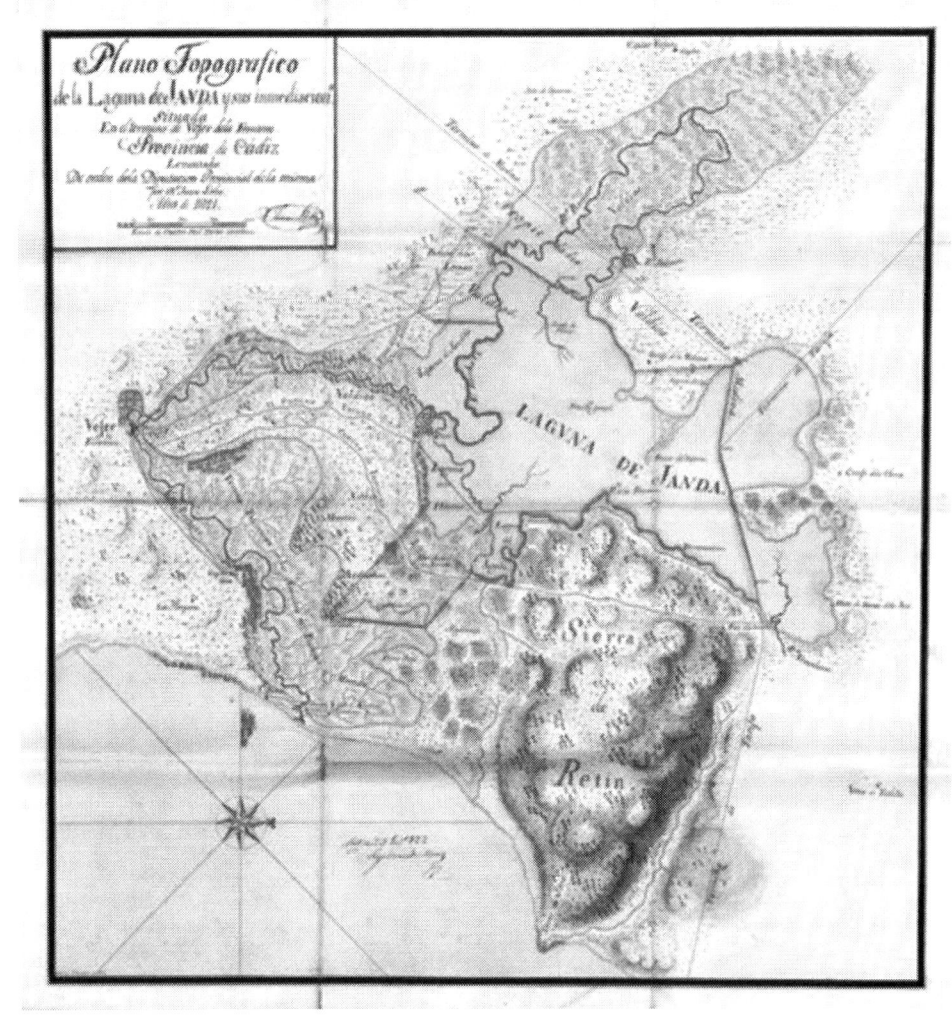

Topographical plan of the Lake of La Janda situated in the area of Vejer de la Frontera in the Province of Cadiz, 1821.

The genetic composition of ancient Iberia was more or less what it is today. When I speak of Celts, Romans, Goths or Moors, I speak only of visitors, intruders, temporary residents. Celt, Roman, Goth and Moor are straws in the wind, passing figures in the ancient landscape, where the first Spaniard opened his mouth to call the beautiful country of Andalucía 'home'.

Chapter 1

Iberia

Homo Antecessor

Neanderthal woman

Before history, there was landscape. But landscape has its own history. In the Jurassic period, 213 million years ago, the age of the dinosaurs, there was only one continent, Pangea. As South America and Africa drifted apart in the Cretaceous period, the Atlantic Ocean rushed in to fill the space. The place which would become Vejer acquired a sea view.

Before the first human creature, there were the sea, the sky, the hill, the river and La Janda lake, 3,700 hectares of linked ponds and marshes, the biggest wetland in Spain. Teeming with fish and home to hundreds of species of birds, it was a perfect home for mankind.

The first early humans appeared on the Iberian Peninsula over a million years ago, in the form of *Homo antecessor*, also called *homo heidelbergensis*, a tough, cannibalistic cousin of modern humans. They settled down around the shores of La Janda, and along the banks of the river Barbate, where archaeological evidence of their presence has been found.

These early cousins hunted with stone tools and lived, on the whole, an out-of doors life, cooking meat and vegetables on campfires. *Antecessors* were nomadic hunter-gathers, moving with the seasons to find food and shelter; they spoke, reasoned and worked with their right hands. The team of archaeologists working at the Sima del Elefante site in the Atapuerca Mountains discovered an antecessor jawbone, evidence of tool making and a 1.2 million year old molar. Chillingly, in view of its owner's dietary preferences, it was described as 'well-worn'.

European *homo antecessor* evolved into *Homo Neanderthals*, a hardy ice-age people who dominated Europe for a hundred thousand years from 130000 BC to 30000 BC. Neanderthals were muscular, intelligent and articulate. They disliked hot weather and followed the cold. Successful hunters, they cooked and ate both meat and vegetables, but they were not anatomically able to throw spears. During the last glacial maximum, Neanderthals retreated to southern Europe, where the most recent evidence of their presence was found in south west Iberia, dating from 24000 years ago. They would undoubtedly have made use of the caves around Vejer, in la Barca and the surrounding area, just as they did in Portugal and nearby Gibraltar. The longer survival of Neanderthals in south west Iberia has led to the theory that they interbred with members of Homo sapiens, and 1-4% of European DNA is now thought to be Neanderthal.

The progress of the human race was sharply halted around 70000 BC, when the mega-volcano Tobo erupted, casting a pall of ash over Asia and producing a volcanic winter which lasted a thousand years. Following this disaster, the number of humans alive on earth was reduced to just a few thousand couples, and all modern humans are descended from these flexible, resourceful and extraordinarily lucky individuals. Around 30000 years ago the first wave of Homo sapiens, descendants of the African branch of Antecessor, migrated to southern Iberia via the Arabian Peninsula, and eventually replaced the Neanderthal families living along the lake and riverbanks.

Like the Neanderthals, Homo sapiens were hunter-gatherers. They lived collectively and apparently without social distinctions, at the mercy of the climate and their own ability to pursue and catch the large animals they preyed upon. They had long, swift legs and excellent imaginations, having already developed language, music and art, as well as a sophisticated self-awareness. Evidence found in El Palmar, on the coast near Vejer, suggests that towards the end of the Paleolithic Era, the people who lived in the area had a religious culture related to the afterlife and the cult of the dead. Although like their predecessors, they were nomads, they often established themselves in two separate areas, one for everyday living, and one as a base for hunting. They made use of the natural materials they found around them, sandstone, shingle and abundant water resources.

Out of these early communities, tribal societies evolved, based on hunting but, including some division into specialist activities, a social structure which created flexibility and the possibility of dealing with hard times by sharing resources.

Between 26,500 and 20,000 years ago the earth froze, as the Last Glacial Maximum took hold. Ice sheets covered North America, northern Europe and Asia. The river Barbate dried and the lake evaporated. The ocean receded. Vejer was barely habitable; a barren rock whipped by frozen winds and buffeted by dust storms. Human life continued in forests, where trees gave protection and scarce food resources were preserved.

Ten thousand years ago, the last Ice Age ended and the men, women and children who had been born in these 'refuges', the small areas where life could still go on, began to venture out across Europe. One refuge in particular, in north-western Iberia, had sheltered a group of curly-headed people who spoke a language resembling Basque. Their descendants moved both south and north, to the westernmost tip of the Iberian Peninsula, and to the western islands of Britain. Commentators from Tacitus onwards have commented on the similarities between the Irish and the people of the Iberian Peninsula, but in recent years their observations have been confirmed by several genetic studies. From a genetic viewpoint, it seems that the Welsh, and Irish are indistinguishable from the people of the Basque country.

The close historical relationship between Spain and Ireland is also revealed in legend. The Irish are said to be descended from an individual called 'Mil Espáine', (Spanish soldier), a descendant of Noah whose sons conquered the nation and gave the Irish the name 'Milesian'. An alternative myth recounts how Hercules, looking for somewhere to hide some sheep he had stolen from Geryon in Cádiz, was seduced by a princess, Keltine, who subsequently gave birth to twins: Keltos, the ancestor of the Celts, and Iberos, the ancestor of the Spanish. As though in acknowledgement of this connection, Irishmen who could prove an ancient pedigree were welcome immigrants to the court of sixteenth century Spain.

In 1913, Juan Cabré, the soon-to-be distinguished archaeologist, arrived in Benalup-Casas Viejas, a few kilometres to the north of Vejer, to investigate reports about the existence of cave paintings in Tajo las Figuras to the east, which local people believed to be very ancient. Scrambling the 10 metres up the rock face to the cave mouth, he noticed shapes in the surrounding countryside which resembled prehistoric dolmens he had seen at other sites. When he finally reached the mouth of the cave, he was disappointed to find that it was full of birds' nests, obscuring the walls. But as he looked more closely, he saw forms emerging from the darkness – the shape of a hunted animal surrounded by humans appearing to dance around it, birds and other animals. He had arrived at one of the most important sites of cave art in Spain.

In the next decade, Henri Édouard Prosper Breuil, better known as Abbé Breuil, a French Catholic priest, archaeologist and scholar, began an intensive study of the cave paintings. The site consisted of eight caves, all containing wall paintings, and a group of dolmens and burial grounds in the immediate area.

The paintings had been made during the Mesolithic Era, the period of transition between the Paleolithic and Neolithic eras around 10000 years ago, when hunter-gatherer societies began to develop farming and walled towns first appeared on the landscape.

The human figures are shown dancing, hunting and leaping; the animals include foxes, snakes and deer. It's clear that the first people to emerge from the Ice Age shelters possessed a complex culture and a rich

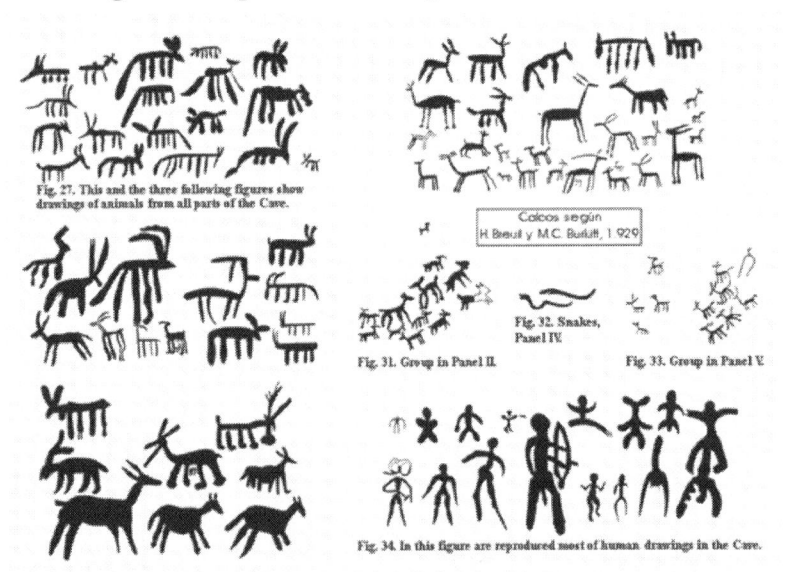

Abbé Breuil's representation of the cave paintings at Tajo las Figuras:

imaginative life. Abbé Breuil's book about the caves, *Rock Paintings of Southern Andalusia: A Description of a Neolithic and Copper Age Art Group* was published in 1928, and is still in print.

The Neolithic period, which lasted from 6500-3000 BC, was a period of explosive human development. Animal husbandry was developed as well as the cultivation of land. The first farmers arrived in Andalucía around 5000 BC, and settlements began to appear in caves or sheltered areas. Man-made caves, abundant in the Province of Cádiz, were a feature of the era, and caves in the Vejer area were inhabited continuously during this period. Red pots found near Vejer, decorated with ochre, predate similar works found in other parts of the Iberian Peninsula, and locally discovered stone tools, made with imported materials, prove the existence of foreign trade.

Remains of the past surround Vejer. At Navaros, burial chambers carved out of rock, have been discovered from the same period, clearly related to cave paintings at La Cueva del Tajo de las Figuras. Some archaeologists have argued that they were bone houses, provided to strip the flesh of the dead before interment. In 1917, a Neolithic tomb was discovered in the Paseo Canalejas in the San Miguel area of Vejer, consisting of a vertical shaft intersected by a horizontal chamber containing two skeletons. The chamber was equipped with two stone hooks, presumably for the worldly possessions of the deceased.

In 1982, agricultural workers discovered a second tomb in an artificial cave at Buenavista, one and a half kilometers from Vejer. Unfortunately the tomb had been looted, and all that was found was a portion of bone on a thin layer of sand, which had formed the floor of the chamber. A ceramic bowl from the same era was also found at the site.

As the new technology of farming took hold of southern Iberia, human destiny changed forever. Changes in farming technology included the plough, land irrigation and the cultivation of wheat, grapes and olives. These innovations required the investment of time and resources, and gradually, society became stratified, with some strong individuals emerging as chieftains, members of a privileged elite.

This change is revealed in the variations between burials, some clearly more sumptuous than others. In Andalucía, however, where resources were not as scarce, the old egalitarian habits persisted. Collective burials continued for another millennium, and lavish grave goods were scarce. Some communities created hill-forts like the one excavated at Millares in Eastern Andalucía, which were used for defensive or residential purposes.

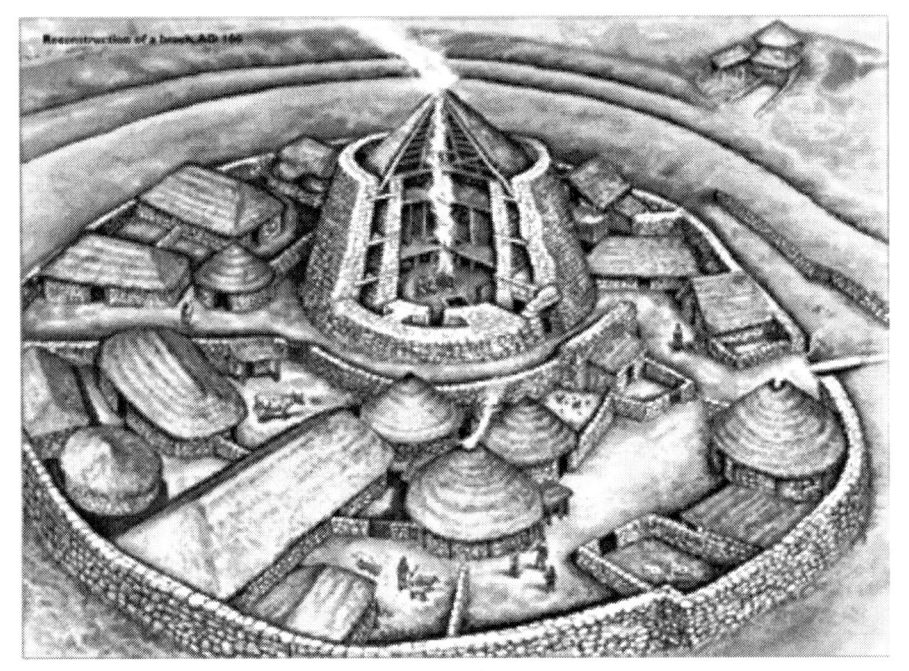

A hill-fort from around 3000 BCE

Chapter 2

Tartessos

3000 – 600 BC

Three-headed Geryon

Tartessian warrior with bee shield

In 1987, as the great project of restoring Vejer's medieval city walls was in progress, workmen made an extraordinary discovery on Calle Juan Bueno. Carefully removing the loose stones of the enclosure, they found another, much older wall. Work stopped while archaeologists investigated the site.

They identified the wall as belonging to the late Bronze Age, confirming what had long been suspected – that there had been a settlement at Vejer long before the written records suggested.

The excavation showed two distinct levels, representing different periods of occupation. The first and most recent contained pieces of pottery from the Turdetanian era, the civilization which had occupied south-western Spain at the time of the Roman occupation. The second, deeper still, had pottery from an even earlier time.

In the period between 900 and 600 BC, the southern coast of Iberia, between the Straits of Gibraltar and the south of Portugal was known as Tartessos, a kingdom with a great city at its heart.

According to mythology, its origin dated from Geryon, the shepherd king whose cattle were stolen by Hercules. Other legends speak of a second Tartessian dynasty, from which we know two names, Gárgoris and Habas. Gárgoris discovered honey and instructed the people of his city in its manufacture and use. His grandson Habas was a civilizing king who gave laws to his people, taught them to plough with oxen and divided the people into seven social classes.

King Argantonus of Tartessos

Tartessos was a harbour city 'beyond the Pillars of Hercules' (Strait of Gibraltar), whose influence extended to the whole of the surrounding area. Its wealth was legendary, partly because of the rich mineral deposits around the Rio Tinto, the iron-stained 'red river', which flows into the Gulf of Cádiz at Huelva. Around 3000 BC, Tartessians began to extract tin from this site, and were able to establish themselves as major exporters of this and other metals.

Tartessian artifacts are recognisable by their geometric patterns and finely worked cast bronze. They show clearly that a rich and sophisticated culture existed in the area during the Bronze Age.

Tartessos is one of the great legends of the ancient world. Biblical sources tell of the trading ships which came every three years to the court of King Solomon, bearing gold, silver, ivory and peacocks. The story of Jonah relates how, intending to flee God's purpose, he took a passage to 'Tharsis.' These written sources and other archeological testimony confirm the relationship between Tartessos and the eastern Mediterranean from as early as the ninth century BC. The base of the interchange consisted of gold, silver and other metals, particularly tin, a material which was abundant in Southern Iberia, and was essential for the production of bronze.

Recent research has shown that Tartessos was a Celtic-speaking civilization whose founders arrived in south west Spain around 5000 BC, as a branch of the Indo-European expansion which had started in central Russia. Once established, they were able to exploit the rich mineral resources of the area to create a wealthy civilization. They colonized and enslaved the local Iberians, and their language became dominant.

Several ancient writers identified the Tartessians as a Celtic people, but a major misunderstanding was created when Greek historian Herodotus stated that the Celts originated from the area around the source of the

Tartessian inscription

Danube. He thought the Danube began somewhere in Iberia, and unwittingly hoodwinked generations of historians into careful theorizing about the Central European origins of the Celts, creating a historical red-herring which lasted for centuries and skewed our understanding of Celtic history.

The first settlers spoke a form of the Indo-European language which is the basis for most European languages, but the dialect they brought with them evolved into the ancestor of the modern Celtic languages, Irish Gaelic, Scots Gaelic, Welsh, Cornish and Breton, as well as several ancient Celtic languages which are no longer spoken.

The Tartessians probably learned the skill of writing from the Phoenicians after the establishment of the trading city of Cádiz; their language, Tartessian, has been preserved on graves and monuments, and we now know that Vejeriegos once spoke a language that we recognize as the ancestor of Welsh, Irish and Gaelic.

Indo-European, society, which came into prominence through its use of the horse and the wheel, had no words for water-borne transport, making it possible to judge the evolution of other, seaborne civilizations from this father-language. It is now understood to be misleading to think in terms of a Celtic genetic identity, as the Celtic languages evolved much later than the original population of Great Britain, but the strong connection between the Tartessian language and modern Celtic is a certain signal that Tartessos was a Celtic-speaking culture. The table below gives a few examples:

Tartessian	Welsh	Irish	English
elu	elw		plenty/gain
kerdo	cerddwr	cerd	poet/ craftsman
ira	gwr	fer	man
melesau	melys	milis	honey-sweet
seta	sedd	síd	seat
sarunna	seren		star

The reason for this connection lies with the exceptional mobility of Bronze Age societies, and the overwhelming importance of the sea in the transport networks of what we now call the Atlantic Zone (the south-west Iberian Peninsula, North West France and the western British Isles.) Because bronze is an alloy made of copper and tin, which are found in different parts of the world, traders developed extensive trading networks to bring the two metals together. The map below shows how the world might have looked to a Tartessian navigator, who would have regarded the ocean as an aid to travel rather than an obstacle.

The great wealth of Tartessos was based on the trade with Britain and Northern France, from where raw materials and finished articles were traded for hundreds of years. Much of the evidence for a Tartessian-British connection comes from Ireland, which developed Bronze Age technology later than the countries of Southern Europe. The spread of the Celtic language from southern Spain is accounted for by the movement of skilled Iberian craftsmen into the countries, and Celtic first established itself as a lingua franca along the west coast of Europe during this process.

Leaving no stone unturned, geneticists have discovered that small Irish mammals such as voles, mice and polecats are genetically related to Iberian mammals of the same type, and bear little resemblance to their English counterparts. They arrived by boat, along with the first traders. In North Wales, a significant migration established several communities around the same time as the first carbon dated copper mine in Llandudno: 1700 BC.

This suggests a considerable business ethic, as does Cicero's comment 'For I think that if I ever make a speech for the state before the Senate, your Tartessian friend will say to me on the way out, 'pay up if you please!'

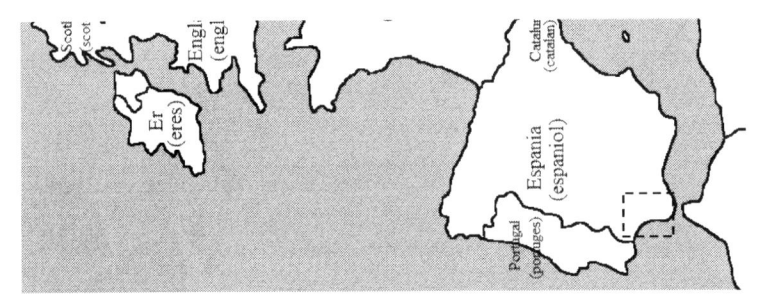

The Tartessian traders' world view

Although the Atlantic trade continued to flourish, by the 12th century BC, the Eastern Mediterranean nations were on the brink of catastrophe as the glittering edifice of Bronze Age Europe shattered, plunging the Mediterranean and near eastern nations into a 400 year dark age. The Egyptian and Hittite cultures, Cyprus, Syria, the Levant and Mycenaean Greece all disappeared under sudden and violent circumstances, and every great city from Troy to Gaza was left in ruins.

The causes of the catastrophe are not clear, but reports of implacable aggression from a group of Northern invaders, described as the Sea People, suggest that groups of central European raiders, fleeing famine in their own lands, made a series of determined assaults on the richer countries of the eastern Mediterranean, possibly joined by mercenaries and dissident slaves.

The sea peoples were a varied group, but genetic evidence shows that some of them arrived from central Asia and the Russian steppes. It is sometimes argued that they were armed with iron weapons, not yet adopted by the Mediterranean cultures. In all probably, the Bronze Age collapse was caused by a combination of social and environmental factors. The process of smelting bronze requires huge quantities of charcoal: the wood needed to build trading ships also helped to strip the hills of their forests. Diminution of resources, possibly exacerbated by drought, seismic activity and volcanic eruptions, culminated in a snowball effect, with violence and rebellion breaking out in all quarters.

When the dust cleared over the former palaces of the eastern Mediterranean, none of its former glories were left intact. Only one city was untouched – Tyre, the trading city of the Phoenicians, who with Mycenaean Greece, had dominated the Mediterranean trade routes for two hundred years. The Phoenicians, not burdened with ideological scruples, did business with the Sea Peoples around the Black Sea, and so bought their protection, while their rivals sank beneath the onslaught. The Phoenicians were left with a clear field, and, given the scale of destruction in the east, looked west for trading opportunities. The focus of their efforts was now the rich mineral deposits of southern Iberia.

At some stage during the 11th century BC, a questing Phoenician ship cruised past the coast of Andalucía, and seeing a plentiful supply of edible-looking creatures on the shore, put in for supplies. They celebrated their discovery by naming the newly discovered land after these small creatures; i-shepan-ham, the land of the hyrax, though the creatures weren't hyraxes at all – they were rabbits. The name stuck, however, and has come down to us as the name for Roman Spain; Hispania.

Around 1000 years BC, the Phoenicians built the city of Cádiz, hoping to establish a trading monopoly on the mineral deposits belonging to the wealthy city of Tartessos. This caused a dramatic change in Tartessian society. Instead of turning to the Atlantic for cultural and trading partners, it began to look eastward to the wealthy countries of the Mediterranean, and trade with Britain gradually came to an end.

The re-emergent Greeks admired Tartessos, and recorded the name of one of its kings, the wealthy Argantonio, who reputedly reigned for eighty years. Tartessian eels were praised, but Greek commentators were less positive about the ferrets, which apparently were large and nasty tempered.

Sometime around 600 BC, the city of Tartessus ceased to exist. The reason for its disappearance is not known for sure; the switch from bronze to iron might have fatally damaged its trading networks, or the encroaching sea may have swallowed it. After the disappearance of the city, Tartessos evolved into Turdetania, considered by the Romans to be the most civilized of the Iberian cultures, possessors of grammar and laws of great antiquity.

Turdetania was a society with many urban centres, including the small but strategically significant hill town of Beser, the castle by the river. Beser's people were true and faithful descendants of the old Tartessian king, Gargoris, who first learned how to domesticate the humble bee, and for many centuries come, the town would bear the nickname 'Vejer of the honey'.

For thousands of years, the location of the city of Tartessus remained a mystery, but in recent years, two possibilities have emerged. Bearing in mind that classical texts described the city as standing between the twin estuaries of a great river, researchers have established the presence of an ancient settlement under what is now the Doñana National Park, at the estuary of the Guadalquivir river, whose second estuary has now silted up and disappeared. Archeological discoveries in the city of Huelva have also established that there was once a large and wealthy Bronze Age city under the present one. At last, Tartessos may have woken from its centuries-long sleep.

Tartessos has all the allure of a lost city, and has been claimed as the site of the city of Atlantis. The theory arises from Plato's location of Atlantis 'beyond the Pillars of Hercules', or the Straits of Gibraltar, and the obvious association of two ancient cities, both now lost. The theory was recently given a boost when a piece of Tartessian pottery was discovered near Sevilla bearing the ringed symbol of Atlantis. Similar artifacts have been found at the site of an ancient pottery in Jaen. Spain is currently number one in Google Inc's index of theories about the location of Atlantis.

Loading a Tartessian ship

Turdetania

Chapter 3

Turdetania

539 - 209 BC

Hannibal

Turdetani flute-player

The discovery in Juan Bueno was not the first evidence of Bronze Age occupation. Several years previously, a team of road repairers had discovered a burial chamber containing human ashes in a ceramic urn. The discovery was not reported immediately, but when archaeologists heard about the find, they were able to identify the pottery urn as Tartessian. This, however, was not proof of a settlement on the site of the present town, and so the discoveries on Juan Bueno were greeted with particular warmth. They were soon outdone, however, by another excavation which put the matter beyond any argument. In 1990, work started on the ancient Convent of the Conceptionistas, which was in serious need of repair.

It soon became clear that a major architectural discovery was imminent. The excavators had found a section of a Turdetanian settlement, with rectangular dwellings, arranged in terraces on the slope of the hill. The houses were built of sandstone, with plastered walls and shingle floors. These houses had clearly been well-supplied with pottery utensils, because many household items were discovered, not only Turdetanian in style, but also Phoenician, illustrating the co-existence of the two communities. Carbon dating identified the houses as belonging to the centuries 4-2 BC, the eve of the Roman occupation, but pottery finds were also made from a much earlier era, and some were dated to 930-790 BCE.

Many of the ceramics were typically Phoenician; plates with fish patterns and other characteristic designs, telling conclusively of trade with the Mediterranean coast, but a large quantity of typically indigenous pottery with the broad stripes typical of Tartessian ware was also found. These relics are now kept in the museum in Cádiz, until the happy day arrives when Vejer has its own museum.

The Phoenicians would not have recognized themselves as such. That was the name the Greeks and Romans gave them, referring to the Murex shellfish they had a monopoly on, the source of imperial purple dye. They called themselves Canaanites, having migrated east from Yemen to an area roughly similar to today's Lebanon. Although their influence was widespread – one man in seventeen in southern Europe can claim direct descent from these enterprising people - in general, they were fair- minded trading partners, and though they were astute and even exacting in matters of business, they did not make excessive demands on the inhabitants of their colonial cities, of which Cádiz was one of the most important.

All this changed in 539 BC, when the Phoenician homeland was captured by Persian invaders. The nearby colony of Carthage, which had been established three hundred years before, became the new base for Phoenician culture, and the centre from which trade and exploration operated. The Carthaginians, however, disliked the laissez faire attitudes of their predecessors, and established their own governments in the colonial cities, with the power to raise taxes. This was an unpopular move, which damaged relationships between Carthage and its colonies.

Turdetanians enjoyed a well-regulated lifestyle and their society had much in common with that of Ancient Greece. According to the Greek geographer Strabo, who lived from 63 BC to 24 AD, they had adopted the Phoenician language of their trading partners; other classical observers claimed that their language descended from Tartessian. In all probability, they were bilingual, or multi-lingual. Vejer, which had existed as an Iron Age hill fort, became more sophisticated, boasting the well-built residences revealed in the excavation, and as a maritime city, benefiting from the fishing and trading opportunities offered along the nearby coast. Around the time that Tartessos disappeared, the round huts of the Bronze Age were replaced by rectangular houses built on planned sites, showing an advance in regional architecture. These houses were often replaced by others built on the same site, as seems to have been the case in Vejer.

The population of Turdetania consisted of two main groups, the Celtici, the native Celtic-speaking people, including the Indo-Europeans and the indigenous people they had conquered during the Neolithic era, now thoroughly assimilated, and the Semitic Phoenician people, the Carthaginian colonisers. Though the Carthaginian group was in the minority, it provided the bulk of the governing class, mainly resident in the cities, while the

Celtici were warriors and workers. Some of the more remote tribes, it was fearfully reported, were highly ferocious. Observers described them as tough, wiry, hardworking and quarrelsome, also remarking that they were remarkably abstemious. The Phoenicians, on the other hand, were dark-skinned, curly-haired and peaceable, their minds firmly set on business and the good things of life.

Although both groups existed in Turdetanian society, the degree of integration was varied. In some of its 200 cities, the two communities lived side-by-side, sharing facilities and socializing freely, while in others, each kept to its own side of town. In Vejer, while the Phoenician group would have occupied the prestigious buildings on the summit of the hill, the space was too limited for complete segregation, and this conclusion is borne out by the mix of pottery found at the Conceptionista site.

The exception to these variants was Cádiz – never a truly Turdetanian city, it remained a vibrant, cosmopolitan seaport, where dozens of nationalities coexisted at all levels of society, and continued to be a law unto itself.

Throughout the Bronze Age, iron had been more valuable than gold, and just as the Bronze Age would be better named the Age of Tin, the Iron Age could also be described as the Age of Steel, because it was not until the adoption of carburization (mixing carbon into iron) that iron became a universal and freely available material for tools andweapons. The result was a culture of violence, during which the Mediterranean region was constantly at war.

By the fourth century BC, although Carthage still occupied the whole of coastal Andalucía, it was facing continual challenges from Rome, which had grown from a small kingdom on the west coast of Italy to a successful and aggressive colonizing nation. Whereas Greece and Carthage had on the whole been prepared to divide the Mediterranean between them, the Greeks to the north and Carthage to the south, the Romans wanted it all. Tensions between these two Mediterranean superpowers escalated, resulting in the Punic (Phoenician) wars which raged intermittently for eighty years, from 264 to 146 BC, the most destructive wars the world had ever seen.

Turdetania, with the great naval city of Cádiz at its centre, could not avoid becoming involved. The Carthaginian empire did everything in its power to control the wealth of Turdetania, imposing taxes, forcibly marrying their daughters with Andalucían chieftains, and using terror when all else failed. Turdetani men were conscripted into the Carthaginian army, and though they were not generally averse to a scrap, this caused enormous resentment. In 219 BC, Hannibal, the Carthaginian general, attacked Saguntum near Valencia, a city allied to Rome, and the second Punic war began. Under Hannibal, the output of the Iberian silver mines was used to finance a standing army, and the majority of Hannibal's soldiers were Iberian or North African.

This war is best known for Hannibal's decision to attack Rome from the north, necessitating the transit of three dozen war elephants across the Alps. Although picturesque and imaginative, this plan was unsuccessful: most of the elephants died, and Hannibal failed to take Rome. We do not know the names of the Vejeriego men who fought for Carthage in this epic conflict, but they would not have been able to avoid conscription, though some Iberians, angry at Hannibal's forceful tactics, defected to the Roman side. In 209, when Hannibal's generals abandoned Cádiz, the Romans moved in. Turdetania was now Hispania Baetica, a Roman colony that would endure for four hundred years.

Roman Spain

Chapter 4

Hispania Baetica

209BC - 479 AD

Marcus Cato

One of the first things the Roman noticed when they first arrived in Turdetania, were the neat, attractive, white adobe houses which clustered together on the hillsides, the forerunners of Andalucía's pueblos blancos. These pretty towns, however, were not always amenable to Roman advances. Although Cádiz had willingly accepted Roman occupation, largely because of the trading advantages it brought, the other cities of Turdetania were less impressed.

The Roman army had been greeted as liberators when they first opposed Carthaginian rule, but after the victory of 209, they began to act more like conquistadores, imposing taxes and restrictions and taking what they could out of the land. In 197 BC, the area called Asta Regia near modern Jerez rebelled, hiring mercenary fighters to attack Roman occupied cities. Given the geographical proximity, it would be surprising if the citizens of Vejer did not also take part in the uprising.

In 195 B.C., the consul Marcus Cato was sent from Rome to deal with the rebellion. Before he left, he promised the senate that 'the war will pay for itself', not the last time an invader would make that pledge. He arrived in Hispania to find the province in full rebellion, and rapidly took control, selling the insurrectionists into slavery. Cato returned to Rome with over 11,000 kilos of silver, 600 kg of gold, 123,000 denarii, and 540,000 silver coins, all of which was taken from the Hispanic peoples during the conflict. Turdetania subsided.

The Turdetanian town of Beser, now romanised to Besaro, became part of the administrative district Caesaris Salutariensis. The occupiers respected local customs as long as they didn't cause trouble, and recruited the assistance of local chieftains to maintain order.

Under Roman occupation, Vejer retained its own laws and customs, and was permitted to go about its daily business as before, but was obliged to pay yearly taxes to Rome. The Turdetanian zoomorphic religion, with its guardian lions, also survived, though as time went on there was a degree of syncretisation with the deities of Rome.

Christianity probably reached Andalucía in the second half of the first century, and legend says that a Vejeriego, Firmo, was martyred in the time of Diocletian.

Whether this is true or not, after the Reconquista, the people of Vejer created a cult of Firmo, who is celebrated by a window in the parish church.

In fourth century Baetica, Christianity was tolerated – later the acceptance of Roman Catholicism prompted persecution of Pagans and the closure of their temples. The Christian church was soon organized on hierarchical lines and Vejer fell into the diocese of Asidona (Medina Sidonia).

During the early years of the occupation, it was customary for writers such as Strabo, keen to stress that the arrangement benefited both sides, to insist that the Turdetani were now completely romanised. Over a hundred years later, however, many of their leaders had not learned Latin and required an interpreter to do business with Rome. A people that cling to their own language for four generations can hardly be called submissive.

In time, however, Baetica did become predominantly Roman, its people fluent in their own form of Latin, and in the first century AD, was honoured by the emperor Vespasian, who extended Roman citizenship rights to all the people of Hispania.

Baetica, whose capital was at Córdoba, was an important Roman colony, supplying the empire with olive oil, garum fish sauce, raw materials and agricultural products, and as such, it was equipped with the best of Roman technology, including roads, sewers and aqueducts. Its coastal resources were also much valued for trade and troop movements.

The Romans exerted their influence through the urban centres, and would certainly have maintained a presence in Caesaris Salutariensis, if not in Besaro itself. Life in a Roman town was generally highly stratified, with slaves at the bottom of the social heap, followed by peasants, citizens, gentry and aristocracy. History does not record what the individualistic Turdetani made of these distinctions.

Vejer and the surrounding area show a high level of occupation in the Roman period. The archeological evidence is generally to be found along the route of the ancient Via Herculea, which passes the area of Manzanete on the east bank of the river Barbate, winds around the hill on which Vejer stands, passing San Ambrosio before arriving at Cape Trafalgar and continuing along the coast towards Sancta Petri. Sections of this road can be seen on footpaths leading from the fair field at La Noria, and on the El Abejaruco footpath.

At Libreros, a Roman villa was discovered by the landowner, who found mosaics a metre under the ground. The site was forgotten for years until in 1973, the Archeological Society in Cádiz began a campaign to recover the mosaics, parts of which are now on display at the museum in Cádiz. As the name Libreros is derived from *Labrillia,* the Latin word for bowls, this building may have been a pottery, whose products were used to pack oil or wine for transport down the river Barbate and through the port of the same name.

Workers frequently find Roman remains on the nearby Cerro (hill) del Abejaruco, on one of whose slopes there is a small necropolis. Near the bottom of the hill, in the Loma Del Chorillo, a Roman kiln was discovered, dating from the first century AD. As with other Roman potteries on the Peninsula, it was located close to a waterway, the River Barbate. For a thousand square metres around the kiln, it is possible to find fragments of coins, pottery, glass and metal, dating the site to two eras – the era of Flavian in the first century and another in the fourth and fifth centuries. The excavation of the Convent church of the *Conceptionistas* in Vejer revealed many fragments of pottery from the first century.

A Roman settlement also existed at Barbate, shipping goods to every corner of the empire.

Roman remains have also been found Patría, La Muela, San Ambrosio, el Tunar and Manzanares. There must have been a settlement in the vicinity of the Sanctuary of La Oliva, where a Christian basilica was erected at the beginning of the 7th century, possibly on the base of a previous construction. The settlement in Patria was certainly an important one, and large numbers of coins, mosaics and other remains have surfaced in the area. One example now hangs in the Reception area of the Hotel Convento San Francisco.

Mosaic at the Hotel San Francisco

The best local example of a Roman coastal settlement now exists at Baelo Claudia near the village of Bolonia to the east of Vejer. The town, which dates from the end of the 2nd century BC, began as an embarkation point for Tangiers in Morocco, but by the 1st century A.D., it had established itself as a producer of tuna, salt fish and *garum*.

The town enjoyed considerable wealth until, in the second half of the second century AD, it suffered an earthquake; this combined with the unwanted attentions of several types of pirate, brought the city into decline. It was abandoned in the 6th century AD, but the site, one of the most complete in Spain, shows a typical Roman town, enclosed by a wall, with its basilica, market, theatre and temple clearly displayed, as well as the industrial areas which supplied its income. While we could expect the nearby hill town of Besaro to be different in character, smaller and with a more military function, the style would have been the same.

By the middle of the third century AD, the Roman Empire was in decline, and was fraught with civil conflict, barbarian invasions and internal strife, inevitably leading to economic decline and political decadence. Trade routes ceased to be secure and invaders from the North began to traverse Hispania, reaching the straits of Gibraltar in 258 AD. However, though cities like Cádiz with a strong trading culture inevitably declined, the social system and structures of the Roman way of life persisted up to the end of the Roman Empire in the 5th century AD.

In 1779, when the current church was built on top of an existing temple at the Sanctuary of la Virgen de la Oliva, a Roman pedestal was found, with a Latin inscription on one of its faces. This is the only Roman inscription which has been preserved in Vejer. It reads 'To her beloved husband, Marco Valerio Numa, of the Galeria tribe, 43 years old. His wife and son and heir raised this monument.' Marco Valerio Numa, whoever he might have been, is therefore the first Vejeriego whose name is known to history.

Larger Roman remains can be seen in Cadiz and Medina Sidonia, but have not generally survived in the town of Vejer. However, a section of Roman road and a kiln used for firing pottery can be found on the Sentido El Alberejo to the north of the town.

Roman kiln outside Vejer.

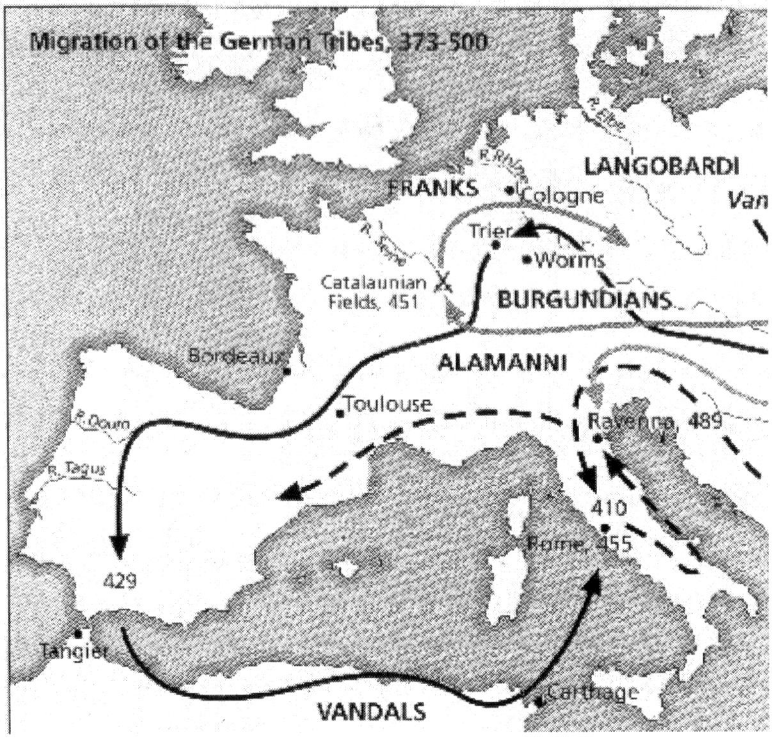
Migration of the German Tribes, 373-500
LANGOBARDI
FRANKS
Cologne
Trier
Worms
Catalaunian Fields, 451
BURGUNDIANS
ALAMANNI
Bordeaux
Toulouse
R. Douro
R. Tagus
Ravenna, 489
410
Rome, 455
429
Tangier
Carthage
VANDALS

Chapter 5
Vandalusia
476 - 555 AD

Odoacer

Justin

At the height of its power, the Roman Empire covered six and a half million square metres of the earth's surface, containing a hundred million people and three hundred kilometers of roads. It was not easily dismantled. Finally, however, it outgrew its strength, and in 476, when dissident Gothic mercenaries, led by Odoacer, deposed the last western emperor, Romulus Augustus, they made official what everybody already knew – Rome was now controlled by Germans. The Western empire expired, while the Eastern branch, based in Constantinople, has been renamed the Byzantine Empire.

In south west Iberia, the power of Rome had been subsiding for a century and hefty walls were constructed to keep out barbarian marauders. In 409, an army of Vandals from modern East Germany overran Baetica, naming the area Vandalusia after themselves. They were ejected a short while later, but took the name with them when they went on to their next assignment in North Africa. According to one theory, it later surfaced as Al-Andalus.

Baetica was not to be left in peace for long. After 476, a contingent of Goths wandered in from their new conquest, Rome, and took command. Cultured Baeticans looked askance at the long-haired despots, and carried on doing things in their own way. But though they were allowed to retain their administrative structures, they were horrified by Gothic law. Homosexuals were castrated, rapists were publicly circumcised and anyone suspected of making magic was cruelly executed. This was not the Baetican idea of a civilized society. In 551, Justin, the Byzantine Emperor, was asked for assistance, and General Liberius was sent with an invading army. He docked at Malaga and made his way to Seville, taking in the town of Medina Sidonia as he went. Vejer was now Byzantine.

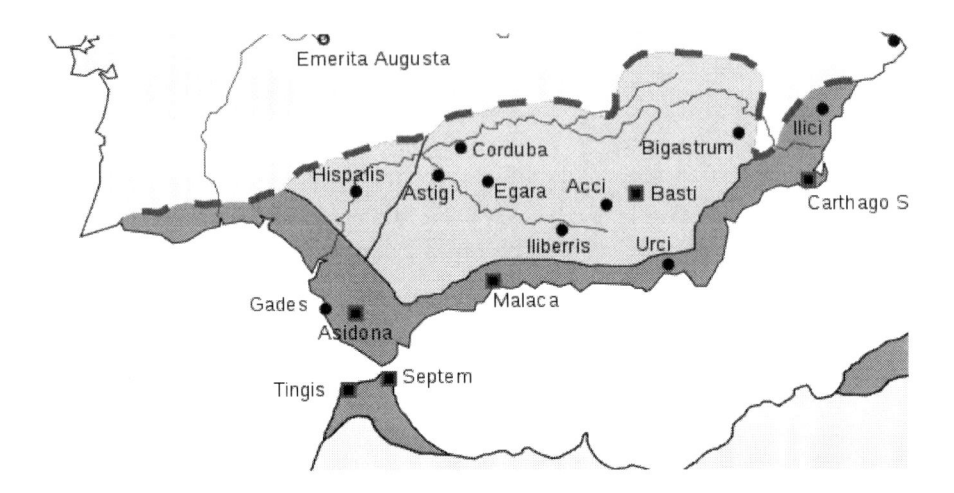

Byzantine Spain, with Medina Sidonia (Asidonia) Cadiz (Gades) and Seville (Hispalis).

Chapter 6

Spania

555 - 572

Gothic Queens

Byzantine rule did not turn out to be much better than its Gothic counterpart, but in any case, Vejer did not enjoy it for long. Byzantine forces failed to hold the border, and the area around Medina Sidonia was recaptured in 572, an inside job facilitated by a servant called Framidaneus, who was a secret supporter of the Goths.

Even while Byzantine rule lasted, borders were porous, and Byzantine and Gothic people mixed freely. In 624, the Visigoths drove the last Byzantine forces out of Spain. The link with Rome was finally broken.

EUROPE
c. 600 A.D.

Chapter 7

Landa-Hlauts

572 - 712

King Reccared 1st

King Teodoracio

The Visigoths, a tribe from the Danube area, had originally been subsidized by the Romans in exchange for providing warriors to fight in the Roman armies. Having helped to subdue a rebellion in Baetica in the early fifth century, they were rewarded with territories in Gaul.

Despite their flowing blond hair and flashy jewellery, the Visigoths were thoroughly romanised, with an effective grasp of Latin. They adopted Christianity, and seemed content to remain in Gaul until the Franks ejected them in 507. They gradually moved into Hispania, displacing the Vandals and Alans and effectively rebuffing the Byzantine invasion. The capital of Visigothic Spain was established in Toledo.

As time went by, the cultural distinctions between Baetican and Goth lessened, and during the next century their identity gradually merged with that of the local Hispanic people. According to Marianne Barrucand and Achim Bednorz, they called Baetica Landa-Hlauts, 'the conquered land' in the Gothic language.

Since their adoption of Christianity, Visigoths had followed the Arian branch of the religion, which denied the idea of the trinity, causing difficulties between them and the Roman Catholic people of Hispania. In 589, however, they were instructed by King Reccared the First to adopt the Nicene faith, and religious dissent erupted.

For most Visigoths, Aryanism was the true religion, and to abandon it in favour of 'Roman Religion' was tantamount to rejecting their identity. It was as if the Protestant population of Northern Ireland had abruptly been ordered to convert to Catholicism, and there was general outrage, with dissenting groups persisting in most communities. Nevertheless, Visigothic society embraced religious tolerance, and a local king, Teodoracio, founded the basilica of La Oliva in 674. Archaeological remains reveal the presence of several different religious cults in the 7th century, in la Barca and in the old town of Vejer itself.

Under the Visigoths, Vejer continued many of the occupations and activities that had developed during the Roman era. Pottery was made in the area and taken down the River Barbate to La Barca, for transportation to one of many destinations along the Atlantic or Mediterranean coast. There was a nightly delivery of fish to the castle at Medina Sidonia.

Though Vejer's own castle can only be confidently dated to the Islamic period, the town itself shows evidence of much older occupation, and the castle must have existed in some form during the Visigothic era, as well as the church. Several archeological remains show the flourishing of religion in the Vejer area during the 7th century. Epigraphs tell of the dedication of the church of Los Santos in Medina Sidonia in 630, and la Oliva in 674, both on the sites of Roman villas and probably replacing previous places of worship. In la Oliva, on the same pedestal as the Roman inscription, there is a Latin inscription which records the dedication of the Visigoth Basilica on the 15th of January 674.

It is also reasonable to suppose that there was a basilica in Vejer itself. Although relics of the Gothic occupation of Spain are few, one dramatic exception remains, hidden in the countryside in San Ambrosio, where the ruins of a Gothic chapel still exist, one of the very few remaining Gothic buildings in Andalucía. An inscription found in the church records its consecration by the bishop Pimenio in 644 AD.

Until 710, Gothic Spain was ruled by King Witiza, but in the same year, a usurper, Rodrigo, carried out a coup and Witiza was imprisoned and killed. Witiza seems to have been a liberal monarch who opposed corruption in the church and recommended that priests should be obliged to marry instead of keeping concubines. He also legislated for the fair treatment of the concubines of the nobles. After his death, it was said that 'Witiza the wicked taught all Spain to sin', a rather tabloid-sounding statement which suggests that Witiza may have been the victim of a backlash from the moral majority. Naturally, he was detested by the Church, which strongly supported Roderick, though the people apparently loved him.

Witiza left two, or maybe three young sons, who were sent into exile in Morocco. However, his brother, Oppas, Bishop of Seville, and some of Witiza's Andalucían supporters conspired with Islamic leader to invade Spain, defeat Roderick and return the line of Witiza to the throne. It was assumed, wrongly, that the Arabic invaders would simply plunder the land and then go back to Morocco.

In 711 or 712, Roderick was defeated by invading Arab and Berber warriors in the Battle of La Janda, also known as the Battle of Guadalete, or the Battle of the River Barbate, placing it within a few miles of Vejer. The Arabic texts vacillate over the name of the location, citing Wadi-Lakka, Wadi Leke, Wadi-Beke, or Wadi Bekke.

Twentieth century historians identified Wadi-Bekke as the River Barbate, and the town Bekke as an Arabic version of Vejer. The battle was the culmination of a succession of invasions, progressively weakening the Gothic defences, which were also Witiza fighting in northern Spain.

Most accounts of the invasion were produced by Arab historians, who vary considerably over the details, but all agree that the Arab general Tariq left from Ceuta and landed at the rock of Calpe, later Gibraltar, which was subsequently, renamed Jebel Tariq, 'Rock of Tariq'. After (according to legend) burning his boats, Tariq moved to conquer Algeciras, then followed the Roman road towards Seville. The date of the battle has been estimated as the 19 July 711.

The armies that met in battle are not reliably described in the surviving records, but there were probably no more than two thousand soldiers on each side. It seems likely that there was disloyalty among Rodrigo's followers: a cavalry wing that had secretly agreed to rebel against him stood aside, giving the enemy an opening. As there was also hostility between Byzantium and Hispania, Byzantine forces may have supported the Moorish attack.

After his victory, Tariq was able to take Córdoba, and then Toledo. In 712, another wave of invaders crossed the straits of Gibraltar and conquered Seville and Mérida. By 714, the whole of Iberia was in the hands of the new power.

Although it seems strange that the whole of Hispania should have fallen into Moorish occupation in only five years, the grip of the Visigoths was never very strong on this former Roman colony, and the 'decadence' of the Visigoths was well-known. Their internal power structures were in disarray. Arabic commentators, attributed their defeat to their sins, and for many centuries it was interpreted as divine retribution.

Roderick's body was never found, and in some quarters he was believed to be still alive, living as a monk. Whatever his fate may have been, Roderick became a legendary figure, whose appearance, like that of King Arthur, was believed to be imminent in the long years of occupation which lay ahead.

After La Janda, the Moorish advance was swift. Nevertheless, as the dust of the battle settled, and Tariq's men pursued the defeated Christians into the sierra, one Northern king survived, limping home to gather around him the guerilla resistance fighters who would make the first tentative steps towards reoccupation.

His name was King Pelagius, and he was the founder of the Kingdom of Asturias, the first Christian kingdom of modern Spain.

D. PELAYO.
PRIMER REY DE ASTURIAS FUÉ PROCLAMADO EN EL AÑO 714. DE CHRISTO: REYNÓ 23. AÑOS: MURIÓ EN EL 737.

Chapter 8

Al-Andalus

712 - 1264 AD

Abdularrahman

'The Christians have forgotten their own speech, and among a thousand of them one cannot find a single one who can write a correct Latin letter to a friend.'
Alvarus, España Sagrada, 9th century.

As the quotation suggests, there was no lack of Christians in Islamic Spain, although as time went by, they were increasingly inclined to read and write in Arabic. Early records show that Christian churches, bishops and other religious features were abundant in the first two hundred years of Islamic occupation.

After Tariq's victory, Arab sources claim that the sons of Witiza, on whose behalf the invasion had supposedly been made, were given a thousand farms each in different parts of the country, carefully calculated to keep them happy, but separate. Their descendants were highly influential in the politics of al-Andalus.

Especially among the ruling classes, there was substantial intermarriage between the Muslim and Christian communities, and the great Abdularrahman III, who ruled el-Andalus for fifty years, was a blue-eyed redhead, being three-quarters Hispano–Basque, and only one-quarter Arab.

The *Muwallads*, people of mixed race, supposedly inferior, were a significant though difficult forcé in society. They frequently rebelled, changed sides when it suited them, and even when they were behaving properly, they annoyed the authorities by converting to Islam and so depriving the public purse of the taxes Christians and Jews were obliged to pay.

The Islamic community was far from united, and there were conflicts between the Shiites in Seville and the Sunnis in Córdoba, as well as an almost permanent revolution in Western Andalucía, while from the north, the rebellions of Christian Omar of Toledo (Ibn Hafsun) almost overthrew the Islamic state between 924 and 933. Maintaining the balance of power was a never-ending process of treaty-making, warmongering and intrigue.

The invaders faced difficulties from the outset. Between 748 and 754, a severe drought ravaged Andalucía. So great was the famine that many Arabs had to retreat to North Africa, passing along a river on the edge of Medina Sidonia known as 'Wadi-Barbat´. Those years of famine have become known in Arabic history as 'the years of Barbate'.

Though Moorish Spain was now a reality, it lacked an effective leader. In 756, however, an Ummayad prince from Syria arrived in Granada. Abd al-Rahman was the son of the Umayyad prince Mu'awiyah ibn Hisham. In 750, when he was twenty, his family was overthrown in a popular uprising known as the Abbasid Revolution. Abd al-Rahman fled Damascus, with his brother Yahiya, to the River Euphrates, dodging the Abbasid riders sent to hunt them down.

Further along the road, the assassins caught up with them again and they jumped into the river. Abd al-Rahman was separated from Yahiya, who panicked and swam back towards the horsemen. The riders begged the princes to return, promising that they would not be harmed. Abd al-Rahman pleaded with Yahiya to keep going: "O brother! Come to me, come to me!" but Yahiya returned to the near shore, where the horsemen killed him and cut off his head, leaving his body to rot.

According to Arab historians, Abd al-Rahman later declared that once he reached the shore, he was so terrified that he ran until he collapsed with exhaustion. He continued to Morocco, from where he reached al-Andalus, where he began to gather support.

He was a tall, charismatic individual, red haired and handsome, and having established his rule, he settled in Córdoba, where he created a modern city with paved streets, lighting, baths, a clean and convenient water supply and gardens, the most advanced urban development in Europe. Córdoba became a focus for intellectual activity, and learning flourished there. The Great Library established by Al-Hakam II contained 400, 000

The great mosque at Cordoba

The Umayyid dynasty founded by Abd-al-Rahman flourished for three centuries, and when it declined, Spain was divided into the smaller city states of Malaga, Seville, Granada, Toledo and Valencia. Christian Spain summoned its resources and began to fight back, but from the fall of Toledo in 1085 to the conquest of the Kingdom of Granada in 1492 was a long, difficult and painful journey.

Islamic Spain was a multi-cultural society, populated by Arabs, Berbers, Iberians of various types and Jews. The Moorish invaders offered tolerance to Judaism, liberty to all slaves converting to Islam, a benevolent taxation system and a religion without theological complexities which was simple to practice. Vejer identified as a Berber city, and after an initial protest, seems to have participated rarely in the frequent rebellions against Muslim rule.

The Vejer of the Islamic era, now known as Bashir, was a typical walled city, with a number of gates, which would have been impressively ornamental, like the present Castle gate. The main gate, probably situated where the Arco de la Segur is now, would have been been wide, with a second, internal door, leading to an open area where the markets were situated.

volumes compared with a mere 2000 or so in Europe's largest libraries, and it was said that in Córdoba books were more eagerly sought than beautiful concubines or jewels. Córdoba's mesquita, or grand mosque, was one of the wonders of the medieval world.

Al-Andalus in 10.35

The most prominent building would have been the Kasbah, a semi-military area surrounded by towers and ornamented with a double horseshoe gateway, situated at the highest point, where the castle now stands.

Bashir would have had a medina, a town centre where commerce and artisan crafts were conducted. From there, narrow steep streets led to the mosque on the site of the current church, built shortly after the town was occupied on the site of an early Christian basilica. The road continued towards the Kasbah via a street corresponding to the current Calle Rosario. The residential areas were probably located around the present Canelejas, or ReyesCatholicos.

There would also have been suburbs outside the city walls, where some of the less choice professions, such as muleteers, fullers, tanners and dyers, who were considered unclean, were obliged to reside. Each street had a Mokadem, a local leader. The town would have had public baths and fountains, but none of these survived the Christian era. A Jewish quarter would also have existed, probably in the same area as the current Judería. There was a cemetery, in the area of the present Plaza de España.

The town would have operated under a well-regulated administration. Public order and cleanliness, water supply and sewers were provided for by the Sahib al-Shurta, while the Sahid al-Madina took care of the town in general, including justice and politics. The Nadir del Habús supervised public welfare. Trade was overseen by the Sahib-al-Suq, and the judge, El Cadi, presided over religious and secular law.

There would have been several mosques, all broadcasting the call to prayer at regular intervals during the day. Friday prayers, however, would have been conducted in the main mosque. The Jewish community would have held prayers on Saturday. Religious holidays were celebrated, particularly the birthday of Mohammed.

Christians and Jews, both called *dhimmi*, paid the *jizyah*, a hefty tax which guaranteed them freedom from persecution, and both Christians and Jews were theoretically allowed to retain their own judges. Relationships between Muslim and Christian were generally tolerant, though Mozarab (Christian) peasants employed on large estates in Andalucía rebelled against their masters on a regular basis.

In the days when a *Pueblo de la Frontera* was known by the Arab name *thaghr*, Mozarabes sometimes defended the border against Christian neighbours. Mozarabes were unlikely to take part in trade or commerce, which they found morally repugnant, but they often migrated north, taking sophisticated Islamic culture with them, and so enriched the Christian cultures of northern Spain.

There is no way of knowing how many Mozarabes lived in Vejer during the Islamic occupation. As a group, they were more prominent in the early Islamic period, and as time went on tended either to migrate north or lose themselves in the melting pot of Islamic Spain. Inevitably, there would also have been a number of mixed-race *muwallads*.

A Christian community must have existed before the Reconquest, because several Christian Vejeriegos were documented in the redistribution of Jeréz in 1262, although it is possible that these residents of Vejer were not of long standing, but had arrived during the power vacuum which existed between the start of the Christian reoccupation and the Crown's final assumption of power.

Vejer acquired its identity during the Islamic occupation. The first written reference to Islamic Bashir occurs in 895, when Abd Allah, the Umayyad Emir in Córdoba, subdued Seville and several other rebellious cities, including Medina Sidonia and Bashir, and subjected them to the authority of the emirate. Vejer was already strategically significant, owing to its situation, and status as a hilltop stronghold, and in the 10th and 11th centuries, these features were developed, with the addition of substantial fortifications. Defences were constructed at los Caños de Meca, improvements made to the Roman buildings in Patría and the aqueducts at St. Lucia, also originally built by the Romans, were extended and developed.

In the mid twentieth century, workers carrying out repairs in the area of the Arco de la Villa discovered several tombs aligned from south to north, on what was the approach to one of the gates to the Islamic city. From this

The ruined Islamic town of Siyasi (Cieza) in Murcia gives a clue about 'Moorish' Vejer

evidence, it is clear that the area was once an Islamic cemetery, orientated towards the East, and the site of the Arco de la Villa was the '*bab maqbara*' or cemetery gate of the city. As time passed, cemetery sites often became places for meetings or recreation, especially after Friday prayers.

The Arco de la Villa was the principal entrance to the town, communicating with the wells at el Corral de Concejo and La Barca, as documented during the repopulations of 1288 and 1294.

Partly because of the force of their ejection, and its relatively early date, the Islamic occupation left few tangible remains. Vejer has no Alhambra or Mezquita. The inner door of the Castle archway, with its horshoe arch and decorated cornices offers a tantalizing glimpse into the architectural beauties the town must once have possessed, but in the smaller towns of Andalucía, the most precious Islamic legacy is probably the four thousand words of Arabic origin which have entered modern Spanish through the Morazabic dialect spoken at the time of the occupation.

The Moorish horseshoe doorway at the castle

Some scholars have gone so far as to suggest that Andaluza, the dialect of Spanish spoken in Vejer, is a hybrid language, part Arab, part Latin, based as much on the ancient dialect of the Mozarabes as on classic Castellano. It is an invisible heritage, but it lives on the lips of every man, woman and child in Vejer, and all the surrounding towns of Andalucía.

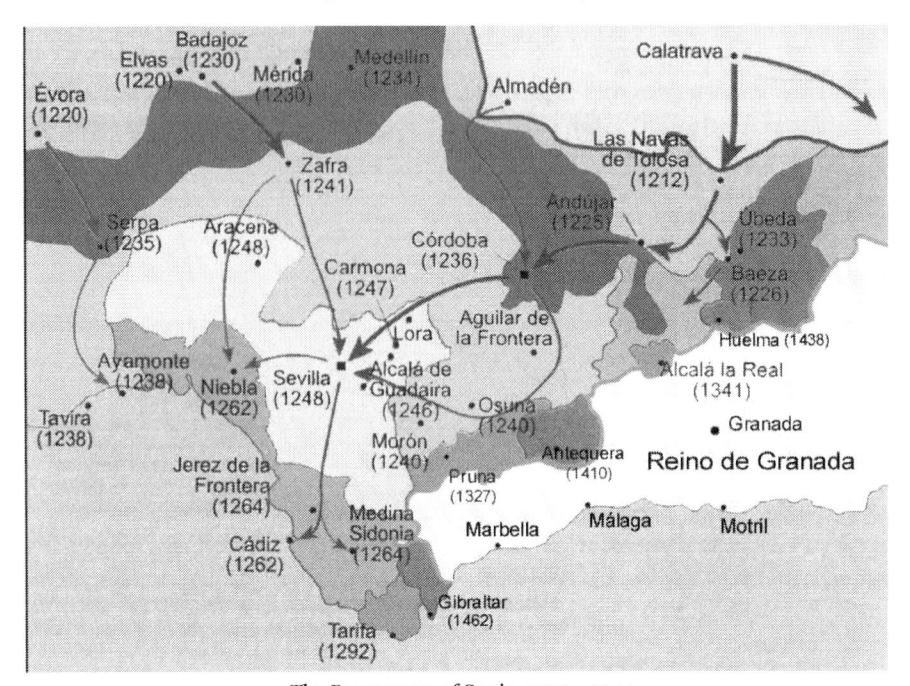

The Reconquest of Spain 1230—1344

Chapter 9

The Reconquista
1264-1492
Narguillén

King Sancho 4

Guzmán el Bueno

Count Pelagius was a reasonable man. Although he had fought the Muslims at the Battle of La Janda in 712, when he returned to his lands in the mountains near León, he accepted their patronage and continued to run his estates under Islamic jurisdiction, accepting this arrangement as the least unpleasant of several unattractive alternatives available to him under Muslim rule.

Pelagius tried to make the best of a bad job for a while, but when, five or six years later, the new governor of nearby Gijon wanted his sister for a concubine, he felt that a line had been crossed, and refused to agree to the arrangement. The Governor, a serial womanizer, saw Pelagius' refusal as an act of rebellion and complained to Tariq ibn Zayad, who was commanding the province from Córdoba. Tariq gave orders for Pelagius to be arrested and put in prison.

Pelagius stopped being reasonable. Like many of his contemporaries, he was beginning to appreciate the difficulties of co-operating with a regime and culture very different to his own. He gathered his family around him and pulled up the drawbridge. Infuriated, Tariq sent a detachment of infantry under General Alkama to flush him out, and to deflect any possible religious justifications Pelagius might claim, the Bishop of Seville also joined the party.

Pelagius, now thoroughly annoyed, had no intention of submitting to Tariq's army. He gathered together a group of Visigothic nobles, all disgruntled after several years of having their cattle appropriated and their women abducted, and they prepared for a fight. They decided to launch an attack on the approaching soldiers from the Covadongas area, where extensive caves would give them the advantage of surprise.

The Battle of Covadonga 722

An Arab chronicler would later scornfully refer to this small guerilla force as 'thirty wild donkeys', but in this case, Arabs were the asses. Pelagius and his men swooped down from the hillsides and scattered the army, killing the general and taking the bishop prisoner. When the remaining soldiers fled, the guerillas followed and attacked again from the rear. The fight was later celebrated as 'the Battle of Covadongas'.

Pelagius was duly lionized as the hero of the episode, and the other nobles voted him their leader, or Prince. The Muslim occupiers, chastened, and more than a little cautious, held back. A decade or so later, exhausted by the rainy terrain and its constant guerilla attacks, they withdrew altogether. In case they changed their minds, Pelagius and his people moved in and constructed heavy duty defences along the mountain passes. The Kingdom of Asturias, the first Christian kingdom in modern Spain, had become a reality.

From this nucleus, opposition to Islamic occupation gradually increased. After 1000, the Moslem caliphate of Córdoba began to break into several smaller states divided by warfare. This provided the opportunity for Christian forces to initiate the Reconquista, led by the Kingdom of Castile which captured the Muslim city of Toledo in 1085.

The Kingdom of Aragón began its own offensive against the Moors in the early twelfth century and an alliance with Catalonia in 1140 furnished additional military power. In 1212, Pope Innocent III proclaimed a full crusade against the Moors and at the Battle of Las Navas de Tolosa on 16 July 1212, King Alfonso VIII of Castile joined his Christian rivals, Sancho VII of Navarre, Pedro II of Aragon and Alonso II of Portugal in battle against the Berber rulers of the southern Iberian Peninsula. This was an important turning point in the *Reconquista*.

The Castilians went on to take Baeza and Úbeda, gateways to Andalusia, while Ferdinand III of Castile took Córdoba in 1236, Jaén in 1246, and Seville in 1248, followed by Arcos, Medina-Sidonia, Vejer, Jerez and Cádiz. By 1270, the Moors were confined to the small Kingdom of Granada in the south of Spain, which they held until 1492 when the Catholic Monarchs Ferdinand V and Isabella I completed the Reconquista by capturing the last Moorish enclave in Spain.

The surrender of Seville 1248

In 1231, the young Prince Alfonzo, whose army later liberated Muslim Vejer and the surrounding territories, took part in a raiding expedition around Córdoba and Seville. One day they found themselves near Jerez, where they where they 'spread themselves against Beger' and 'took whatever they needed'. This is the first appearance of Vejer in the chronicles of romance, and the earliest record of the Christian conquerors.

Although the fall of Vejer to the Christians in early 1264 was recorded by the Primera Crónica Gral, we are not told whether the town was regained by conquest or capitulation. Whichever it was, the event did not go unchallenged. In June 1264, the Mudéjares, Muslim Spaniards, fought back in a general revolt, supported by the emir of Granada, Mohammed 1 and troops from North Africa.

The rebels seized the castle in Vejer and put the entire garrison to the sword. Alfonso's army conquered Vejer on the feast day of the Transfiguration, August 6th, naming a new church in honour of the occasion, and Muslim families were expelled, forfeited their goods and cattle to the invaders, and were obliged to flee to Granada or Morocco.

Fragile and vulnerable though the reoccupation of Vejer seemed to be, there was an urgent need to repopulate the area. With its Muslim occupants expelled, it was a ghost town, its future still to be invented. The land had to be cultivated, and an absence of residents might encourage the former occupants to return. Though the majority of Muslims had left Vejer, either forcibly or by choice, bandits and guerillas still roamed the nearby hills, ever-alert for an opportunity. Vejer had been Muslim for five hundred years, approximately the same length of time that Europeans have inhabited North America. To its Muslim community, Andalucía was the land of their fathers.

Arab occupation had produced four distinct, though overlapping, strands of population. The Mozarabes were Christians, mainly descended from the Visigoths or their predecessors, the Romanised Baeticans. They spoke a version of Latin called Latino, not to be confused with the Ladino spoken by Sephardic Jews. The Mudéjares, on the other hand, were Moslems who agreed to convert to Christianity after the Reconquista, Arabic speaking people whose conversion was often pragmatic rather than heartfelt. They were usually agricultural workers or artisans. The Muwallads were people of mixed race. The majority, however, consisted of Muslims of North African or Arabic descent, who were not willing to convert.

Jews, though numerically significant, maintained their own culture. Although there is no record of the relative composition of the people of Vejer after the Reconquista, we do know that when the Christian repopulation was formalised, about a third of the population was described as 'Andalucían', mainly Mozarabes or Christian Muwallads.

Reoccupation of the area was not achieved overnight, however, and the Muslim stronghold in Patria remained occupied until 1271. Muslim Patría seemed peaceful, but once Vejer had been conquered, it made no sense to tolerate the presence of an enemy stronghold in its hinterland, however small, and Patria was forcibly evacuated. The destruction of the villa must have been absolute, because it was not mentioned in the redistribution of Vejer a short time afterwards. El Libro de Alcázar, written in the XVI century, contains an account of the final destruction of the stronghold.

Once a peace had been signed with the Muslims, Alfonso was in a position to implement his reoccupation plan. For strategic reasons, the town of Vejer remained a military garrison for a short while, but the surrounding areas were repopulated with Christian settlers, mainly people from Castile and León, the Christian north.

Vejer regained its Christian culture and Romance language. The Reconquista had made large areas of land available for distribution, and in order to attract colonists, farms, homes and favourable tax arrangements were offered, especially to those who had distinguished themselves in the military campaign to retake this part of Al-Andalus. Large estates, or latifundias, were established, which eventually led to the demise of small private landowners, creating social and economic problems which persist to the present day.

The first item in the repartimiento was the disposition of the castle and surrounding town of Vejer. In general, settlers were allocated parcels of land: three yugadas for hidalgos, two for knights and one for members of the lower orders. (1 yugada =approximately 1,400 square metres.) Some selected knights received considerably more, sometimes as much as 20 yugadas. Not all the land was allocated immediately, in anticipation of further settlers; in 1293, the process was repeated and all the available land was allocated, though modifications were made as late as 1318.

Apart from the 30% of the population which was described as Andalucían, 28% came from Castille and the rest from other places in Spain and

Europe. Most of the new vecinos were farmers, labourers and tradesmen, though some held military rank, and some were clerics. Among the occupations listed in the redistribution document were three gardeners, a miller, a shoemaker, a roofer and a butcher. These were generally enterprising and pioneering people, though like many immigrants, they may also have been in retreat from problems at home.

In 1269, Alphonso X granted grazing and other agricultural rights to the citizens of western Andalucía in order to foster prosperity and economic growth. Besides doing something to avoid the excessive concentration of property in the hands of a small number of landowners, this action encouraged the settlement of immigrants from Castile and Northern Spain. The local nobility was initially reduced in numbers, but their ranks were reinforced by some low-ranking Castilian nobles, the most prominent of which were the Amaya and León Garavito families. The Amayas settled first in Jerez, but by the 14th century, established themselves in Vejer.

The León Garavitas arrived from the North around 1450, apparently following a scandal in their town of origin, in which a 'maiden' was compromised. One of the biggest landholders at this time was Hernan Guillén, the first Mayor of Vejer, whose family arrived in 1288. Guillen's presence in the town was remembered down the centuries, because even in documents from the 19th century, the town was sometimes called 'el cerro (the hill) de Hernán Guillén', or more colloquially, 'Naguillén', the last oral trace of the man who was Vejer's first Mayor.

In 1274, the Emir of Granada requested help from the Merinid sultan Ibn Yusuf in Morocco to combat the Castilian expansion, and offered Tarifa and Algeciras as points of disembarkation for the invading forces. The ensuing struggle between Christian and Muslim lasted 75 years, years of suffering for coastal villages like Vejer, which endured countless attacks from the Muslim armies. Only five days after the Merinid army disembarked, Vejer was sacked, and the invaders rode towards Jerez, burning the crops in the fields and laying everything around them to waste. In 1278, the castle and fortress of Vejer were attacked again, and the surrounding countryside ravaged. Enough was enough, and Alfonzo negotiated a truce which allowed the Christian garrison to return and remain in Vejer unmolested. In 1284, however, Alfonso X died and the raids began again. The violence of 1285 was appalling, and every town between Barbate and Guadalete was sacked.

At the end of 1285, the new King Sancho IV (el Bravo) and Abu Yusuf agreed another truce. The Merinids kept the beaches of Tarifa, Algeciras and Gibraltar, and the assurance that the Castilian king would not interfere with them. In exchange, Sancho received the assurance that in future, the towns and villages along the border would not be molested. Nevertheless, the violent and unstable political situation might have endured for much longer if political issues in Morocco had not obliged the Merinids to seek a treaty with the Castilian monarchy. Sancho came under pressure to consolidate the political and military position of Vejer, and in 1285 ceded to the Military Order of Santiago sovereignty over Vejer, Medina Sidonia and Alcalá los Gazules.

As a consequence of this decision, Vejer would have ceased to be an independent town and became a feudal possession, and the Knights of Santiago would have taken charge of the town and its surroundings. For some reason, however, the Knights did not take possession of any of the three towns, and when Sancho ordered the redistribution of Vejer in 1288, no member of the Order appeared among the new owners.

When the treaty with Castile expired, the Merinids renewed their incursions into Spain and in 1291 Vejer was besieged for three long and desperate months. The siege was eventually broken by Sancho IV, but while it was in place, some recent settlers abandoned their holdings and left the town. To reward those who had endured the siege and kept the walls intact and town safe from invasion, Sancho granted the people of Vejer several privileges, intended to reward them for their efforts and in December 1293, he sent engineers to improve the fortifications. The most exposed areas of the Castle were repaired and strengthened, but the town walls must have been considerably weakened during the siege, because the cost of repair was 4.900 maraviedies, considerably more than any other town on the area. (A maravedié was approximately 3.8 grams of gold.)

Vejer was also granted 14000 maravediés to make improvements, followed by another 3000 for additional expenses. In addition, 11600 was granted to the town to maintain the 'velas' who patrolled the walls and fortress, the 'atalayas' who manned the various lookout towers, and the groups of vigilantes who rode the country areas, protecting farms and goods in transit. These defences formed a protective web, operating in concentric circles around the fortresses which constituted the nucleus of the system.

The total cost of providing these defences in Vejer was 39.664 maravediés. In 1293 and 1294, Vejer received 179 cahices of wheat and barley (1 cahice = 666 litres). Finally, a considerable sum was made available for the armed men who were recruited in defence of the area.

The medieval population of Vejer was biased towards the military, with 36% registered as 'knights' of one kind or another. The remainder consisted of peasants or tradesmen, with a very much reduced share of society's wealth. Between them, they owned about 30% of the land in the area, while the nobles and the officials of the Church represented privileged minorities. Social mobility was rare. The poorest class of all, the paupers, lived in want, in a constant state of insecurity. At the end of the 15th century, there were 200-300 people in Vejer dependent on public charity.

Alonzo Peréz Gúzman was born in León in 1256, and early documents suggest that he was not Spanish, but a Moor, though his history was edited in the sixteenth century to satisfy the conventions of Christian Spain. He was appointed general in charge of Tarifa by Sancho IV of Castile, and in 1296 he defended the town against the siege of the Moors and the Infante Don Juan, Sancho's rebellious brother.

Gúzman's son had been placed under the care of Don Juan who threatened to kill the boy unless Gúzman surrendered the city. According to legend, Gúzman rebuffed the demand with dramatic words: according to one rendition,

"I did not beget a son to be made use of against my country, but that he should serve her against her foes. Should Don Juan put him to death, he will but confer honour on me, true life on my son, and on himself eternal shame in this world and everlasting wrath after death."

Gúzman then threw his own knife down for the besiegers to use in killing his son. Gúzman was rewarded by large grants of crown land, and in 1309 he helped Ferdinand IV of Castile capture Gibraltar from the Moors, who had held it since 711. In 1445, one of his descendants, Juan Alonzo de Gúzman, count of Niebla, was made Duke of Medina Sidonia. The addition "El Bueno" to the family name was used by several of the house, which included many statesmen and other powerful individuals.

Vejer's fortunes took a decisive turn in 1307, when the Crown transferred lordship of the town to Alonzo Pérez Gúzman, in exchange for the villages of Zafra and la Alconera and the remission of a debt of 56000 gold crowns owed to him by the crown. Clearly, Vejer was held in high esteem by both parties.

Between 1297 and 1307, Gúzman became a key player in the defence of the Frontera in his role as undisputed leader of the territory between Tarifa and Sanlúcar de Barrameda. After his death in 1309, his descendants followed his example, making every effort to defend their manor. While Castile was embroiled in the second phase of the Reconquista, the house of Gúzman, lords of Vejer and Sanlúcar, continued to flourish. In the future, the fate of Vejer would depend on the vicissitudes of this noble family.

The late fifteenth century was dominated by the campaign of the Catholic monarchs to overthrow the Kingdom of Granada. Vejer was turned into a recruiting and provisioning centre for the war effort, dispensing horses, arms and men. Captain Bartolomé de Amaya, the Vejeriego Mayor of Jimena, acquired fame during one of the raids of 1480. Having set out with 120 lancers to take the town of Marbella, he found himself surrounded by 400 horsemen and 2000 Moorish foot soldiers, who, after blocking all the roads and passes with trees, prepared to take him and his men prisoner.

Having refused assistance from a Captain Luciano Marrufo, who had ships in the bay, Amaya gave battle, invoking the name of Santiago, the patron saint of Spain, whose day it was. Mounted on a white horse, holding his sword in one hand and the cross in the other, he charged through the enemy ranks, killing many and taking others back to Jimena as prisoners. His action was popularly viewed as miraculous, and when he died in 1515, he was honoured by the construction of a chapel in the parish church, dedicated to Saint Bartholomew.

The conquest of Granada in 1492 brought about radical changes in Spain's social and political structure. After ten years of fighting, and months of secret negotiations, a treaty was agreed in November 1491, and Christian soldiers occupied the city in January of the following year. The Catholic Monarchs then faced the difficult task of unifying a set of kingdoms with different customs and allegiances to three different religions.

Initially, the Muslims were treated leniently, but the Sephardic Jewish population was less fortunate. Three months after Granada's fall, an expulsion order was issued for any Jew not accepting Christian baptism. This was partly done in deference to popular anti-Semitism, though the confiscated property of the expulsees no doubt proved beneficial to the monarchy, which happened to be bankrupt. Within four months, most of Spain's middle classes had left for the Levant, or elsewhere in Europe. It is said that in some ancient Sephardic families, old keys to their Spanish homes, long ago demolished, are still handed down from generation to generation.

In Vejer, there was a Jewish quarter of some significance, and it is assumed that some families were forced to go into exile. In a list of knights from 1511, the surname of a convert appears, perhaps renamed to reflect his occupation: 'Corchero, (cork worker), new Christian' who preferred to receive baptism, rather than go into exile. After the Reconquista, the Catholic Monarchs initially pursued a policy of colonization in North Africa, for which they required control over the ports of Cádiz, which passed to the crown in 1492, and Gibraltar, which Duke Juan Alonzo exchanged for Gaucin in 1502. Vejeriego Francisco de Mendoza, a relative of the de Amaya family, became the Mayor. However, the effort to maintain the Reconquest and the new developments in the Americas meant that only the island of Melilla came into Spanish possession, and when the Crown once more turned its attention to North Africa, it was too late.

Sometime between 1485 and 1489, the Muslim warlord Mawlay Ali ben Rachid married a Vejeriega Christian called Fernández, who converted to Islam and adopted the name Zuhra.

As ben Rachid had been born in Granada and received his military training there, the couple may have met in Spain. Ali took his bride to live in Chefchaouen, though the legend that he built the town in imitation of Vejer to ease her homesickness has no foundation in fact. Their two children, Mawlay Ibrahim and Sitta al-Horra, both became prominent citizens and leaders of their community, but Sitta al-Horra was a remarkable woman for her time.

After marrying Al-Mandari, an older man who had been the governor of Tetuán, she took charge of the running of Chefchaouen, greatly increasing her power through the death of her husband and the progress of her brother, Ibrahim. No other woman in the history of Morocco has exercised such sovereign power as she did. She was skilled in the arts of politics and war, and in September 1540, joined with the Algerian pirate Kara Mami in an attack against Gibraltar which produced copious booty and a good haul of prisoners.

Lal la Zahra

The Sultan of Fez asked for her hand in marriage, provoking the jealousy of her family, who conspired against her, and she was obliged to retire to Chefchaouen, where she lived to a great age. In the mosque there is an unadorned chapel which, according to tradition, is the last resting place of the Vejeriega Lal la Zahra and her daughter Sitta al-Horra.

While the skeleton of Vejer had been put in place, its present beauty and elegance were still a long way off. The reconquest remained precarious, and enemies did not give up easily. From now onwards, Moorish raids, pirate invasions, pillage and kidnappings were the price that the new inhabitants would pay for the defence of their land. Vejer was now Vejer de la Frontera.

The Puerta Cerrada, for centuries closed to keep out pirates.

The Mayorazgo tower gave a panoramic view of the coast and the land below.

Joris Hifnagel's engraving of Vejer, 1575

Chapter 10

Vegel

The early modern age: 1500-1700

King Ferdinand of Aragon

Queen Isabella of Castile

The Torre del Mayorazgo, which is open to the public during the hours of daylight, is approached through the double patio of the Casa del Mayorazgo. From the top, a large sweep of coastline is visible, including the coast of North Africa.

This vista, which would have been even wider before the nineteenth century, when a new era of construction obscured the coast to the West, allowed watchers to spot approaching pirates from a great distance, to ring the tower bell and set all the others bells in town in motion and to gather its people within the protective town walls before the intruders were seen off by the local guards. Thanks to its position at the top of the hill, Vejer was able to grow into an urban centre while coastal towns remained undeveloped. The town's modern history begins here.

The final defeat of the Kingdom of Granada and the discovery of the American continent by Christopher Columbus in 1492, paved the way for Spanish expansion, and in the following centuries, Spain established the first global empire. After the Reconquista, establishing Visigothic ethnic identity became a priority, and creative heraldry flourished, with many pedigrees either dredged up from the past or completely invented. The Spanish devised the idea of 'blue blood' – a nobleman demonstrated his pedigree by showing the blue veins visible under his pale skin, proving that he had no Moorish blood.

Despite the initially generous treatment of Spain's Moorish inhabitants, after the Reconquest, opinion rapidly turned against the Mudéjar population and from 1502, Moors were obliged to convert or leave Spain. By the mid 1500s, the use of Arabic was prohibited, and people with Moorish blood became second-class citizens, or at worst, persecuted minorities. The Inquisition, which had been set up in 1480 to regulate the conformity of converts, stepped up its efforts, and suspected all those who failed to drink wine or eat pork.

The most spectacular development of this era was undoubtedly Christopher Columbus' voyage to the Americas, which led to the eventual colonization of the continent. Although Europeans had probably made landfalls on the American continent before, none of them had attempted a takeover. The Catholic Monarchs, on the other hand, were ready for expansion.

By 1492, Spain had colonized all the Canary Islands except Tenerife, providing a useful point of departure for the Atlantic crossing, and Columbus, an awkward-mannered Genoese with some useful maritime experience, including piracy and shipwreck, was certain that a route to China and Japan lay to the West. He had sailed to Africa as part of the Portuguese expansion there, and had also worked as a cartographer. After years of lobbying, he was given the modest sum of two million maraviediés (a recent royal wedding had cost 6 million) to mount his expedition. Andalucían municipalities were asked to provide supplies, including a substantial allocation of wine, presumably the fortified type from Jerez.

In 1492, shortly before the departure of Christopher Columbus, Vejeriego Bartolomé de Torres was in jail in Palos de la Frontera for the murder of Juan Martin, the town crier. Alonso Clavijo, another citizen of Vejer, with some of his friends, attacked the prison and freed the prisoner. They were then faced with the problem of what to do with the guilty Torres.

Knowing that Columbus was in need of a crew, they signed Torres up for the ship's company. Clavijo himself sailed on the flagship, the Santa Maria. When the ships returned to Spain, Torres pleaded for clemency and received a pardon in view of his services to the Crown. His goods, which had been confiscated, were also returned to him. Nothing more is known, however, of Alonzo Clavijo, though a Pedro Clavijo, presumably a relative, appears among the list of 'gentlemen of quality' in Vejer in 1511.

Columbus was aware that the caravel, a small, lateen-rigged vessel, was more effective in open waters than the much larger full-rigged ships generally used for trade. At Palos de la Frontera, near Huelva, he provisioned three vessels, the Niña, the Pinta and the Santa Maria and with the assistance of Captain Martin Alonzo Pinzón, recruited 80 men to sail with him. The voyage from La Gomera (Canary Islands) took 33 days, during which the credibility of his mission was stretched to breaking point. They made land at Long Bay, now part of the Bahamas, and were intrigued by the local residents, and in particular by their habitual nudity.

On returning to Spain, they presented Europe with the first European outbreak of syphilis, which occurred in 1494 when French troops besieging Naples caught it from Spanish mercenaries. Captain Pinzón himself died of the disease soon after returning to Spain. The conquistadores, of course, took plenty of deadly diseases in the other direction, including malaria.

Spanish possession of the American colonies was confirmed by the Pope in 1493, and another, larger, expedition was mounted. The first settlement was established in Hispaniola, and in 1512, Vasco Nuñez de Balboa settled Darién in modern Panama. Thirty years after Columbus' first voyage, an Andalucían crew, captained by Henry Magellan, a Portuguese explorer, would take on the first voyage around the world, proving what had been believed for centuries, that the earth really was a sphere.

From the 16th century to the 18th, numerous Vejeriegos and other Andalucíans made their way to the New World, either clandestinely or as part of official expeditions. Until the mid 16th century, women were not permitted to travel to the Americas, but when this prohibition was lifted, many men called their families to cross the Atlantic and join them in their new habitat.

As Spain entered the modern age, Vejer, Christian for over two centuries now, was a stoutly walled town, with a population of 5000 people, a castle at its highest point, a church and a clutch of houses and workshops of which only fragments now remain. The Plaza de la Villa, on the east of the town, was surrounded by official buildings, and would be clearly recognisable as today's Plaza de España. Its use as a military parade and training ground would be less familiar. Some ancient buildings still remain from this era, notably the Cilla, which is now part of a hotel. During the next century, monasteries and other religious buildings would begin to make their appearance in the town, and the church would be extended.

Sixteenth- century Vejer possessed all the trades that go to make a thriving town; shoemakers, carpenters, ironworkers, builders and millers among many others. Most trades were represented by guilds, of which the first to emerge was the shoemakers. The primary source of income for all citizens was agriculture, though as time went by, and the population grew, there was a shortage of wheat, and grain was sometimes imported to feed the population. Vejeriegos took part in commerce, exporting textiles and agricultural products such as honey and wheat, both overseas and within Spain. The town was supplied with seven kilns for the production of earthenware vessels, as well as six watermills, two inns and a brothel.

All of this should have amounted to a peaceful and settled existence, but the wars were not over yet. The ejected Moors, angry at their expulsion from an eight centuries- old homeland and bitter at the treatment of their counterparts still in Spain, now embarked on a three-century campaign of retribution. Their new kingdom was the high seas; history has named them the Barbary Corsairs.

Not only was the coastline infested with these pirates; the line between legitimate trade and piracy was indistinguishable. Piracy was, in fact, well-established even before the conquest of Granada. On June 13 1478, the courts confirmed a sentence against Antón Bernal, which had been brought against him by Fernánd Goncáles de Tarifa, a vecino of Vejer, for attacking and capturing a cargo of provisions from Seville, destined for Vejer. Bernal, a slave trader and merchant, was respectable enough to have been appointed an alderman of Cádiz. He was not punished for the theft, merely ordered to pay 70000 maravediés, the estimated value of the cargo. Although some corsairs undoubtedly viewed themselves as jihadis, avenging the treatment of fellow Muslims and insults to their religion, piracy soon became an industry, supported by governments, who also demanded some of the profits. The corsairs benefited from the expertise of British recruits like Jack Ward, who turned pirate after losing his job in the British navy.

Although the corsairs' main business was piracy, capturing and looting sea-going vessels, they also remorselessly raided the coastal villages of southern Europe. They were slave hunters, roaming as far afield as Ireland, and on one occasion at least, Iceland, but the main focus of their efforts were the coastlines of Spain and Italy. One of their most famous captives was Miguel Cervantes, the author of Don Quixote, who was captured by pirates on his way home from the Battle of Lepanto in 1575 and remained a captive for five years. He attempted to escape five times before being ransomed.

Vejer was the defensive centre of this stretch of coast, and unlike many other towns, whose defences were flimsy to say the least, Vejer applied good management and imagination to the task of confronting the pirates. The Dukes of Medina Sidonia, who had a great deal invested in the local fisheries, were the most active in the business of keeping the corsairs at bay, but the council also worked hard to maintain the town´s defences in good order, and at one point took the controversial step of selling communal land to pay for increased security measures. The corsairs, who were inclined to advance silently at the dead of night, were hard to resist. Vejer's position on the hilltop gave it a considerable advantage, but the centuries' long closure of the south gate, the Puerta Cerrada, was a wise precaution. This would have been an easy spot from which to enter the town, as the deep cleft of the Barranco de Almarez, now below the Plaza de la Paz car park, would have given the raiders some cover. The Mayorazgo tower, with its panoramic view of the coast, was also an important factor in the town's defences; when pirates were spotted, the prolonged ringing of the bell would alert everybody in the vicinity to the risk of a raid.

Vejer's defences never failed, and Vejer did not suffer a major pirate raid. Unlike many coastal areas, which remained undeveloped until the pirates were finally exterminated in the eighteenth and nineteenth centuries, Vejer survived and owes its uninterrupted history to the effectiveness of its defences at this time. Nevertheless, when King Felipe II's inspector, Louis Bravo, visited Andalucía in 1577, he was horrified at the restrictions fear of piracy imposed on the people, finding them unwilling to leave the town's precincts at any time except the height of the afternoon.

Many Vejeriegos were captured in small- scale raids: when Martín Sanchez and Martín de la Cruz were captured in Zahora in 1590, they were taken to Marrakech, where they were put to work on public building projects. When they arrived, they discovered a small community of Vejeriegos in the same position, ready to offer help and support. The same thing happened in the middle of the 18th century when the monks of La Merced sent a commission to Tetuán where they discovered that at least four compatriots were captives there.

It is estimated that about one and a quarter million Europeans were captured and enslaved between the fifteenth and seventeenth centuries, and though this figure does not compare with the twelve million victims of the transatlantic slave trade, it is nevertheless a substantial number. Arab-owned slaves had to be replaced frequently, as they were often castrated or otherwise prevented from having children, and as with their African counterparts, frequently died in transit or from diseases they had no resistance to. Slaves might be used as sex workers, soldiers, galley slaves or manual workers, though the wealthier captives were usually ransomed, another useful source of income.

Vejeriego captives were not forgotten by their families. Alonso Moreno left more than 100 ducados in his will to pay for the rescue of his son; Bartolomé González mortgaged his house to pay the 150 ducados needed to ransom his grandson. One Franciscan monk spent 13 yrs in captivity and even the united efforts of his entire family were not enough to ransom him. Eventually, his brother in law mortgaged a house on the square of San Francisco. Martín Roman, the brother of another captive, mortgaged his slave, a woman called Lucía, and her three children. It's difficult to imagine that he was not aware of the irony of this.

Slave-owning was a constant feature of Vejer society, as it was everywhere in Spain. Many white slaves were descendants of Eastern Europeans who had been enslaved during the Middle Ages, when the word 'Slav' first replaced the Latin 'servus'. There were more slaves in Seville than in any

A drawing from "The History of the Indies of New Spain," Diego Durán's account of the conquest of Mexico (circa 1581).

other Spanish city, understandably in view of its importance as a port trading with Africa and the Indies, but the practice of owning slaves was almost universal among the wealthy.

In 1492, the Duke of Medina Sidonia owned 95 slaves, 40 of whom were black; in Vejer generally, during the sixteenth and seventeenth centuries slaves numbered around 250 at any time, including children born into slavery. Most slaves were engaged in domestic work, though some were made to work in fishing and agriculture. Slaves were routinely baptized, regardless of their previous religious affiliations. Some eventually found freedom, either earning their release in recognition of hard work, or buying it. While enslaved, however, they were often considered by others as non-persons, marginalized and sometimes despised.

The practice of domestic slavery was made possible by a clause in the law which allowed for slave- owning in times of war, though many slaves were women and children, unlikely to be effective on the battlefield. Initially, many slaves were Muslim captives from the defeated Kingdom of Granada, but in 1570, a Moorish uprising was defeated in the Alpujarras, south of Granada, resulting in the enslavement and dispersal of tens of thousands of individuals. Some African slaves were also acquired through the Portuguese colonies. Mistreatment of slaves was forbidden in theory, (which did not stop it occurring), but for most wealthy people, keeping slaves seemed quite natural and the practice was not questioned.

Along with the development of an empire came the emergence of a transatlantic slave trade. In 1502, Juan de Córdoba of Seville sent one slave to the new colony; only eight years later, King Ferdinand of Spain authorized a shipment of 50 African slaves to be sent to Santo Domingo. By the end of the century, thousands of slaves were being traded by the Spanish empire and transported from Africa to the Americas without setting foot on European soil, but despite the cruelty of this practice, and the misery it generated, it would be two centuries before a serious discussion began about abolishing this practice.

Feliciana Moreno was born in Angola in the late 1640s. While still a child, she was one of many of her fellow countrymen and women to be captured by Portuguese slave traders. In order to fit her for employment in a Christian household, she was taken to the Island of Santo Tomé, off the western equatorial coast of Central Africa, where she was baptised and given a Christian name and education.

When Feliciana's education was considered complete, she was shipped to Faro in Portugal, where she was sold, and remained for several years before being purchased by Cristóbal Cortés, an ensign and slave-trader, to work in his holding in El Puerto de Santa María, near Cádiz. After some time, she was sent to Tangiers, where she worked in an inn. She was then sold to Cristóbal Valdés, a wealthy householder of Vejer, where she rediscovered an Angolan friend, Luisa María, now also a slave. In 1669, Feliciana requested permission to marry Pedro Chacón, a 29 year old slave belonging to Cristóbal Muñoz Cruzado. They both applied to the Vicar, who had known Pedro all his life, for permission to marry.

Since Feliciana had only lived in Vejer for a short time, she was asked to present evidence that she was not already married, and Cortés, now resident in Vejer, affirmed under oath that she was single, adding that he had been dealing in slaves for years, and that in his experience, married slaves always declared their spouses in the interests of staying together. His testimony was supported by Juan Esteban, a sailor who had met Feliciana in Tangiers where she worked in an inn, and knew her to be single. His employer, Cristóbal Pérez, had brought her to Vejer to sell her on behalf of Cortés. Luisa María also testified that Feliciana, whom she had known since childhood, was single,.

Boat skeletons at Barbate, final destination from la Barca de Vejer (photo : Tamsin Carey)

Feliciana's story, which has come down to us through the records of this appeal to marry, is an example of the vicissitudes many slaves had to endure, but we can also rejoice that at the end of her travels she found a fair-minded master, a loyal friend, and, it is to be hoped, a loving husband.

Continuing the tradition of trading which had started with the Tartessians, Vejer was both a producer of exported wares and a transit point for goods from other places. Shipments were either transported via the roads established by the Romans to Cádiz, Medina Sidonia or Gibraltar, or, more often, along the River Barbate. The river port at La Barca ('The Ferry') de Vejer had traditionally provided an embarkation point for goods and passengers, but around 1550, improvements were made which, over the following century, made it the hub of local trade, allowing the Dukes of Medina Sidonia to control imports and exports and collect levies accordingly.

The caves of la Barca were described by a contemporary observer as large enough to shelter hundreds of men, which even allowing for a traveller's exaggeration, suggests that they offered ample opportunities for storage, as well as stabling for a substantial pack of mules. Most of the goods which passed through the area went by water, and La Barca was an essential element in the flourishing trade in tuna. La Cuesta de la Barca, the path which leads to the Plaza de España, provided the shortest route into town. Other traffic, travellers from the north, cattle and wheeled vehicles, used the road network.

One of the chronic problems of the age was the nobility's intrusion into the rights of the people. The aristocracy, the equivalent of today's giant business corporations, were continually trying to increase their holdings and democratic sentiment was notable by its absence. However, as often happens, the tension between the house of Medina Sidonia and the people of Vejer brought forth a popular hero, and one of the town's most beloved historical figures.

When the Gúzman family was granted seigniorial rights in Vejer after the Reconquista, the agreement did not allow the noble house free rein in the administration of the area; on the contrary, the rights of the people were carefully and clearly protected. However, as time went by, the nobility began to abuse their privileges. Although agriculture was the main source of income in the 15th century, much of the land granted by the Crown to the people of Vejer for pasturage had been appropriated by the Dukes for the cultivation of wheat. Much of the profit from local fisheries also went to the ducal house.

As the 16th century advanced, Vejer's economy came under increasing pressure, until in 1535, the situation became unbearable. The people of had repeatedly requested the return of the rights originally granted them by the Crown, but their demands were ignored.

Meanwhile, Juan Alonzo, the current Duke of Medina Sidonia, was busy enclosing public land for his own private use, imposing levies on agricultural production and monopolizing public utilities such as ovens and mills. Worst of all was the limiting of public access to farmland which had been enjoyed as communal ground since the repopulation of Vejer – the Hazas de Suerte.

Matters came to a head when a tax on wine was announced. Juan Relinque was a talented individual who had been appointed to the position of trustee procurator the previous year. He quickly realized that the Duke was not recognizing the rights the people were entitled to according to the royal charter by which the Dukes of Medina Sidonia administered the town. Juan Relinque officially expressed his rejection of the new demand, but the estate dismissed his document. Supported by a number of fellow citizens, Relinque took his complaint to the Royal Chancery at Granada, requesting protection for his plea against the Duke.

A royal decree was issued, instructing the seigniorial authorities to respect his right of appeal. In December, Relinque presented his first demand, denouncing the Duke for the tax on wine, and challenging sales taxes on other goods, such as linen, on the grounds that since the Repopulation, Vejer had been entitled to the privilege of free trade.

The citizens of Vejer argued that having paid the statutory ten percent to the estate, they were not liable for further charges, and claimed that Relinque had been unjustly dealt with by the authorities. The Duke, apparently prevented by arrogance from seeing the writing on the wall, continued to maintain that the estate was his, and he would do what he wanted with it.

Nevertheless, support for Relinque and his followers continued to grow, and the Duke appealed to Granada for the right to punish the rebels. On Corpus Christi day, 1536, the town crier announced on behalf of the estate that communal lands were to be sold to pay estate expenses. Relinque and some of his supporters, meeting in the Plaza de España, confronted the estate office, causing 'scandal and commotion'. Relinque and his people were removed to Sanlúcar de Barrameda and imprisoned there. In November of the same year, the Duke's Procurator requested that the prisoners should remain under lock and key.

However, Relinque was permitted to leave jail in order to plead his case, and far from being intimidated, as the Duke presumably intended, took up the cause with renewed enthusiasm. In May 1537, a royal decree recognized six separate abuses which had been carried out by the Duke.

Not yet satisfied, Relinque continued to press his case, despite an attack of cold feet on the part of some of his supporters, and obtained permission to proceed with a demand for fiscal equality, on the understanding that his case would be prosecuted for the general good, and not for the benefit of any individual.

During this period, several attempts were made to intimidate Relinque and his followers. Faced with the unaccustomed expenses that Relinque´s demands inevitably involved, some powerful families in the town found themselves out of pocket, and attempted to resist the changes. The authorities, however, were prepared to make no exceptions, and ordered them to pay.

Finally, the Mayor, Tebedeo Velázquez, and several other wealthy citizens, surprised Relinque as he was walking through the churchyard, and threatened him. Relinque replied coolly that he merely sought justice, and Velázquez retreated to his house in a fury. During the next four years, Relinque and his supporters pressed for comprehensive reforms and a definitive shift in the balance of power. Their strength was the legality of their claims.

Although in 1307, Fernando IV had given the administration of Vejer, with its castle and fortifications, and its existing and future population, to Alfonso Pérez de Gúzman, this did not imply that Gúzmán had proprietorial and seigniorial rights over the town. As part of the agreement, Gúzmán had been bound to observe existing property rights and privileges.

In 1539, Relinque presented the courts with a demand for full restitution of all rights, judiciously expressed in fifteen different points. The Duke responded with bluster, repeating his assertion of ownership, and showing complete ignorance of the law. Evidence of Fernando's decree was produced, and the Duke's arguments were dismissed. Years later, he was still muttering about 'time immemorial' and 'ancient laws and customs.'

The Duke's party, aware that the point was lost, attempted to stop the process by an agreement with the people of Vejer, and collected some signatures in their support. In 1542, the people of Vejer went back to court to challenge the agreement, which, as Relinque pointed out, was divisive. The court agreed that no agreement could cancel out the rights of the citizens of Vejer, but the issue rumbled on until 1565, when Relinque´s interpretation of the law was finally ratified. By this time, both Duke Juan Alonzo and Relinque himself had died. In 1566, the judges of the King's court issued a condemnation of the ducal house of Medina Sidonia, and ratified all fifteen points of Relinque's plea of 1536. Although the Dukes dragged their feet when it came to putting the decrees into effect, making further rulings necessary in 1569, and even as late as 1627, the point was won.

Juan Relinque García died in 1554. He comes down to us as a Robin Hood of his time, one who used the law to defend his people's rights against a grasping aristocracy. Little is known about him, but what we do know suggests a man of conscience and a firm will. Although he seems not to have had children of his own, in 1541, he adopted a foundling child, a girl whom he named after his wife, Leonor. The girl is not mentioned in his will, suggesting that she died young.

Juan Relinque was clearly a man of parts, a skilled and intelligent interpreter of the law, and an obstinate defender of justice. He was also a man of religion, whose final wish was that he should be buried in the parish church of El Divino Salvador. His bequests were small, but included a few vines, some land, an ass and eight doves. His legacy, the freedom and prosperity of the people of Vejer, is incalculable.

The Dukes of Medina Sidonia were not financially ruined by the new arrangements and continued to be the richest family in Spain, with significant influence on the monarch and his government. Alfonso's grandson, Alonzo, commanded the Spanish Armada in 1588, and was disgraced when it failed; his subsequent withdrawal from public life had a negative effect on trade in the area.

Joris Hofnagel's drawing of Vejer, published in 1575, shows a view of the town taken from Buenavista, where the windmills now stand. As there are no trees on the hillside, a common feature of fortified towns, the walls are clearly visible, and seem to be intact, and from this angle no houses appear outside the walls. Half way down the hill, the Gallardo well is clearly marked. A road which corresponds to Los Remedios leads out of town, and the Hermitage of los Remedios is shown. Its main archway has been preserved and stands in the centre of the road on the way into town. The church tower dominates, though it has a taller spire; it was rebuilt and shortened in the second half of the 18th century. Next to the Church is the gate of La Segur. The castle and the convent of the Conceptionistas are visible, as is the Tower of the Homenaje, which no longer exists.

With the conquest of Granada now in the past, and the risk of pirate attack tempered by excellent observation points, the growing town of Vejer de la Frontera began to spill out of the city walls and into the surrounding areas. After some final modifications in the fifteenth century, the walls were developed no further. Some important buildings, the Convento de la Merced, and the first Convento de San Francisco were built outside the walled enclosure and in the Plaza de la Villa, the nobility began to enjoy the corrida, bull running, mounted on beautiful and expensive horses. Although the great buildings of the eighteenth century were still in the future, with every year that passed, Vejer became more like the town it is today.

The baroque doorway of the Casa del Califa Hotel on the Plaza de la España

The Taking of Gibraltar

Chapter 11

Andaluzia

The French Century

1700-1800

Charles II

Felipe V

In 1701, following the death of the decadent Hapsburg King Charles II, King Felipe V of the French house of Bourbon ascended to the throne of Spain, and 'The French century' began. Matters were complicated, however, when the Austrian Archduke Carlos presented a similar claim. The resulting War of the Spanish Succession was confused further by the intervention of the British, who took the opportunity to seize Gibraltar, then realized that their best interests did not lie in an alliance with Austria and hastily changed sides.

The war continued until 1713; Spain lost its European territories and Britain held on to Gibraltar, but the French Felipe retained his throne. Nothing much was achieved in this epic confrontation and diplomacy would probably have served the purpose better. F

Felipe's Bourbon régime undertook the reform of Spain with enthusiasm, transferring trade with the Americas from Seville to Cádiz in 1717, and rationalising the tax on exports. In response, Spain became defiantly and flamboyantly Spanish, asserting its separate identity in a flurry of bullfights and ostentatious religious parades, not at all discouraged by the bans on such activities regularly issued by the Crown. The divided regions of Spain (with the exception of Catalonia, which exploded in bloody revolt when its ancient privileges were revoked in 1714) now began to present a united front. Spain acquired an army, a national anthem and a flag.

One immediate result of the war was that the British occupied Gibraltar in 1704, since when the rock has remained a British dependency. The attempts both to retake this, and retain the Spanish colony of Ceuta guaranteed Vejer a return to the quarrelsome state of previous centuries. During the 18th century, Vejer took on its current and characteristic form; in 1700, however, many of the town's most notable buildings were still to be constructed.

Although the population in Spain generally had declined during the 17th century, in Vejer there seems to have been little change, and during the 18th century the population rose to 6500. The Dukes of Medina Sidonia continued in their role as feudal overlords, but other local gentry, the Amayas and the León Garavitos, died out or merged with other noble families as their male lines disappeared. There were about a thousand working families, ranging from skilled artisans and traders to labourers. About 400 people lived by begging or received alms from the Church, roughly eight percent of the population. Slavery, however, had virtually disappeared, not so much through moral principle as the scarcity of slaves brought about by the peace with Morocco and the domination of the more lucrative Atlantic slave trade.

As always, the Church showed a strong presence, with over a hundred assorted clerics, including the monks of the Convento San Francisco and the Conceptionista nuns. The town boasted five churches, three of which were attached to convents, and a handful of smaller places of worship, known as hermitages.

The Inquisition had been active during three centuries, during which it came to represent a dead hand on the nation, suppressing all progressive ideas and challenges to the status quo. The liberalizing influence of the French was firmly resisted, and the Inquisition deployed all the powers at its disposal to oppose progress. At a time when the Enlightenment was spreading throughout Europe, Spain was in danger of remaining in the Dark Ages. 'Spain is a thousand leagues from Europe and ten centuries from the eighteenth,' one critic wrote.

Catholicism was deeply entwined with popular superstition, and witches, miracles, spirits and portents were enshrined in religious belief. Terror was the Inquisition's principal weapon; dissent was banned and books burned. In 1776, eight thousand prohibited books were destroyed in Cádiz alone, though the fact that so many prohibited books existed does suggest a substantial opposition. Although in general the people of Vejer lived entirely under the influence of the church, dissenting voices were occasionally heard, such as that of Lorenzo Sánchez, a thirty three year old Vejeriego stonemason, who, accused of having asserted that he did not believe in Heaven or Hell, or the virginity of Mary, was swiftly dispatched to prison, despite a comprehensive account of his religious bona fides given by his defending lawyers.

Vejer's dealings with the Inquisition were tainted by rivalry between the Convento San Francisco and the parish church, who were both inclined to interpret matters in their own way. Tensions grew acute in 1786, when a dispute erupted between the Commissioner of the Inquisition, Don Pedro de Medina y Soto, and the monk Pedro Montesinos against the Vicar and two of the parish priests concerning the conduct of a religious occasion.

In January that year, the office of the Inquisition had informed their commissioner in Vejer that they would shortly publish a General Edict of Faith. To announce the edict, a religious parade was arranged, with music, horsemen and local dignitaries, all presented to their best advantage, and the Edict was duly published from the pulpit of the church. Strong statements were made against the followers of Mohammed, Moses and Luther, and other heretics, and the occasion seemed to pass off successfully. The Vicar and curates were startled, therefore, to receive a letter from Seville the same evening, threatening them with excommunication and a hefty fine for obstructing the work of the Inquisition.

It transpired that the authorities had received a denunciation from the monks of the Convento. This being made public, a crowd of people marched to Don Pedro's offices, where they beat upon the doors in fury. The following day, a tablet left beside the church's supply of holy water announced that the comisario had been excommunicated. Civil commotion duly followed, and though the excommunication was pronounced invalid, the dispute was pursued through the ecclesiastical courts, where it took all the efforts of the judicial process to unpick the knot of envy and resentment which had accrued around the issue.

Morality in 18th century Spain was focused on heterosexual relations, and extramarital sex was punished by exclusion and disgrace, though a judicious wedding could expunge most sins. Even the clergy were not exempt from investigation should their behaviour seem suspect. Though it was not unheard of to anticípate a wedding, or even to precipitate one which had not been intended, open fornication was not tolerated, and malefactors were liable to find themselves in prison.

Several cases were recorded in which men were punished for sexually exploiting women, usually after promising marriage, but where the marriage vow was fulfilled, the man was exonerated. In more serious cases, the court in Granada could be involved, or the man's goods taken in punishment. Women who transgressed, however, received the more subtle punishment of loss of dignity, and possibly the forfeit of their marriage prospects.

Where marriage was honourably offered, there still might be obstacles. Fathers controlled their daughters´ choice of spouse, and defended them from unsuitable attachments. Girls were not allowed to marry slaves, the sons of slaves, gypsies or men of mixed race. Certain professions were also considered undesirable, and the sons of midwives, butchers and drovers were shunned by decent families. Male immigrants were less particular, despite moral disapproval, and there are several cases of local women of colour marrying outsiders, but the reverse never occurred, and even girls from other areas were bound by strict conventions regarding their choice of Vejeriego partner. Fathers, of course, were not always reasonable, and when their prohibitions were ill-founded, the young couple was able to appeal to the Vicar for a dispensation to wed.

In 1761, Vejeriega Luisa Pérez asked her father José Pérez for permission to marry José Gallardo, but having an objection to her choice, Pérez refused to give his consent, and registered his decision with the diocesan authorities in Cádiz. Having heard Pérez' objections to the young man, the diocese made an order to the Vicar of Vejer, requiring that Luisa should be removed from her father's home to a place where she could make her own statement without parental pressure, and he in his turn consulted the Mayor, asking him to meet that night at seven and bring two ministers with him.

A committee duly formed, consisting of the Vicar, the Mayor, and three other persons of authority, as well as Gallardo's legal representative. Luisa was requested to put on her *manto* and other respectable coverings and present herself at the hearing. The Vicar asked Luisa if she had promised to marry Gallardo, and requested some proof of their pledge. Luisa produced a scarf that Gallardo had given her, and explained that she had given him a ring in exchange. The Vicar had already collected the ring from Gallardo, and Luisa was able to identify it. The marriage was duly authorized, though the records do not comment on the quality of family relationships thereafter.

Vejer was still an unequal society in the eighteenth century, and though the law applied to rich and poor alike, the wealthy and high-born were in a better position to avoid the consequences of their actions. Even murders might be excused if the culprit were well placed in society. In 1744, for instance, when Pedro Cano Lobatón killed Benito Sánchez, his father and brother obtained a pardon from Sánchez´ widow on the grounds that he was 'a member of a prominent family´, though the widow also accepted a sum of money in compensation.

In 1773, Vejer experienced a devastating earthquake; 'At at five o'clock this morning,' the Mayor of Vejer, José Perez Rendón y Doncel, wrote on the 12th of April, 'over this town, God brought down upon us the fury of his wrath, with a violent and formidable earthquake which left in a ruinous state many of its buildings, all its churches and a large number of houses'. The terrible Lisbon tremor of 1755, whose tsunami caused devastation in Cádiz and disrupted the fishing in Barbate, was still a recent memory, but the effects of the 1773 quake were not widespread, suggesting that Vejer was at, or very close to, the epicentre.

Master builders Francisco Gutiérrez Afanador and Sebastián Macías were appointed to survey the damage and their statement was given under oath. They reported extensive destruction. A crack had opened up between the castle and the church, the majority of buildings were damaged, and a hundred and fifty houses had collapsed in ruins. The tremor had caused severe damage to the church, including the collapse of the bell tower, virtually destroyed the Church of the Conceptíon and partly demolished the roof of the Franciscan convent. Wells were blocked, creating a public health hazard, and parts of the Judería area had more or less crumbled into dust. It seemed that the entire area was in danger of obliteration and several smaller hermitages, such the ones at Vera Cruz and San Sebastian were in ruins. The two bridges at la Barca were only usable by pedestrians and tragically, the main arch of the ancient Gothic chapel at San Ambrosio had also collapsed.

As a result of the tremor, many people abandoned their houses and businesses, and there was considerable looting, deplored by wealthy citizens such as Manuel de Elvira, the administrator of the tobacco monopoly who had more than 10000 reales stolen from his house. Although detailed records of damage to private houses were not kept, most of them were damaged to some extent. On the Calle Sancho side, for example, the crack which opened up in the wall of the Casa de la Mayorazgo is still discernable, and the Casas Capitulares on the Plaza de Españaalso succumbed, because their walls were made of earth not stone.The castle, Rosario church and the towers and walls were unaffected, as was the Casa Tamarón.

The big question was who was going to pay for the damage? The council took immediate action to clear away the buildings which were on the point of the collapse, but repairs to the town´s major buildings had to wait two years, while the church authorities considered the town's appeal for funds. The Ayuntimiento took on the responsibility for repairing the Chapter house, whose roof had collapsed, but the Church was told to take responsibility for its own property.

Eventually it was decided that Judería and the Church of the Conception should be united and fortified by the construction of three arches, now one of Vejer's icons. Many private houses were damaged beyond repair, but the Casas Capitulares were eventually rebuilt. The chapel of San Sebastian was given a new roof, and the Santa Cruz hermitage was rebuilt, though with a slightly reduced floor area. As a result, the Calle de la Iglesia, now José Castrillón Shelly, was altered to run straight up from the Arco de la Villa, whereas before it had to take a zigzag path to arrive at the hermitage. The Veracruz hermitage itself survived until 1820, when it was turned to another use.

Several other streets had been affected by the earthquake, either cracked or covered by fallen stone. La Cuesta de la Barca was cleared up, as was La Fuente. Other access roads were made accessible and the La Barca bridges were repaired. On Calle Nuestra Senora de la Oliva, and Marqués de Tamarón, some old buildings were cleared away, making the streets wider.

The blackest and most disturbing aspect of this tragedy, however, is the absolute silence that exists about the human casualties. An earthquake which occurs at five in the morning and destroys a hundred and fifty houses must necessarily cause many deaths, and more injuries, but the parish register contains no record of any burials, and there is no mention of the injured being cared for, orphans fed or bodies, living or dead, being brought out of the wreckage.

The Convento arches were built after the earthquake Nor do we hear of epidemics caused by the disruption of the water supply. We can't tell if the looting was sparked off by greed, opportunism or genuine shortages of food and other supplies. Either the authorities were so callous that they cared only for damage to buildings or the extent of the slaughter was so great, and so woefully mismanaged that to put it on record would have been a cause of shame.

The earthquake marked the final phase of Vejer's entry into the modern world. The new houses were healthier and more convenient than the old ones and the final touches were put to the town's unique profile with the new bell tower and the elegant Judería arches.

 Both before and after the earthquake, some grand houses were built to accommodate the local nobility: the Casa de Tamarón, the Casa Naveda (the House of Widows) and the Casa Castrillón. The new Convento San Francisco also dates from the eighteenth century. The old town we see today is largely a product of this episode, an eighteenth century village, its narrow streets winding calmly between protective walls.

Allegory of the Constitution of 1812 by Francisco Goya

El Tempranillo

Rafael del Riego

Chapter 12

'The land of Jesus, within two steps of Paradise.'

(Prosper Merimée, Carmen)

The Nineteenth Century

Merimée's description of Andalucía may have been justified, but at the start of the nineteenth century, the two steps needed to reach Paradise were still extremely large ones. The big story of this era in Spanish history is the struggle between the forces of liberty and reaction as the emerging working class pitched fury and revolt against the equally intransigent and repressive ruling classes, and a growing body of liberal progressives fought to create a Spanish democracy. As a result, universal male suffrage was granted in 1869, though women did not get the vote until 1933.

The century began violently, with the Battle of Trafalgar in October 1805, during the Napoleonic wars. In May 1805, Napoleon Bonaparte, invoking the Treaty of San Ildefonso, requested Spanish support in the war between France and England. Spain had a policy of neutrality, but was unable to avoid becoming involved. The battle was fought at Cape Trafalgar, near Los Caños de Meca. Vejeriegos watched the conflict with interest and growing horror, later reporting the outcome to the Cádiz press.

This battle marked the end of Spanish naval power and the emergence of British naval supremacy. Spain´s subsequent inability to defend her American colonies led to a general decline as the Bolivarian revolutions in

South America took on momentum. Mexico's independence was recognised in 1821 and in 1898, Spain relinquished all claim of sovereignty over Cuba, the last colony.

By 1808, the people of Spain were tired of the French, and their resentment came to a head, when the French army was attacked in a series of murderous riots on the second of May. The insurgents were duly shot on the third, but though the French regained control, the Spanish people would henceforth demand a voice. The subsequent conflict, known in Britain as the Peninsular War, was named the War of Independence by the Spanish.

The French, determined to make their presence felt, marched into Vejer at the beginning of 1810, established the Convent of La Merced as their headquarters, ejected the nuns, and immediately began to make requisitions. They soon reduced the old building to a state of dereliction. The local authorities were obliged to supply enormous quantities of grain and forage for their horses, and the leader of the civic authorities was taken into custody.

Given the impossibility of leaving their homes and occupations, the local people could only hope to wait out the storm and covertly make their unwelcome visitors' lives as difficult as possible. They did not have long to wait. In the autumn of 1810, The British sent the Duke of Wellington to liberate Spain, the French were defeated near Chiclana in March 1811 and with inspired collaboration from Spanish guerillas, the French were ejected in 1813, having withdrawn from Andalucía in 1812.

The conflict seems to have produced Vejer's first investigative journalist. Miguel Salcedo Nuñez recounted how, disguised as a shepherd, he travelled to Retin, where he came across a British detachment, which he helped to negotiate a passage to Conil and Chiclana. He was detained for nine days in Jerez on suspicion of giving help to the enemy. After his release, he joined his wife in Tarifa and took a passage to Cádiz, now the nation's capital through the opening of the Cortés, where he hoped to obtain a passport from the authorities. He was denied the right to live in Cádiz on account of the high number of refugees currently in the city, placing a strain on the

Salvador Viniegre: Promulgation of the Constitution 1812

infrastructure. However, he was allowed to remain in the city for fourteen days, before returning to Vejer to write up the experience. There is little written evidence of the veracity of the story, but it has entered the oral history of Vejer, and is frequently cited as an example of the town's involvement in the war.

The removal of the Cortés to Cádiz (via Seville and Puerto Real) produced the most decisive political event of nineteenth century Spain. Realising that Spain would be difficult to govern after the withdrawal of the French, the Cortés contemplated two possibilities: a return to the old regime, or a written constitution. The progressive majority demanded a constitution.

The 1812 Constitution established the principles of universal male suffrage, national sovereignty, constitutional monarchy and freedom of the press, and supported land reform and free enterprise. It also guaranteed the citizenship of all overseas Spanish citizens and redefined the colonies as provinces of Spain, with equal rights.

The Constitution reflected many of the principles of the French Revolution, and would have reduced the Crown and Church, the twin pillars of Spanish authority, to mere sidelines in the national polity. This was too much for conservative Spaniards, who were no mood to appreciate anything that came out of France. The ´Cádiz liberals' gained little more than a set of powerful enemies, and when, in 1814, King Fernando VII returned to the throne, the liberals were persecuted, imprisoned or forced into exile. The genie, however, was out of the bottle, and during the following years, Spain saw a succession of mini-revolutions against Fernando's doctrine of absolute monarchy. The general unrest culminated in the Civil War of 1820 to 1823, led by an officer called Rafael del Riego.

Rafael del Riego y Nuñez was born in Asturias, the land of Pelagius, where many a Spanish rebellion has been fomented. He graduated in 1807 and joined the Army, fighting bravely in the War of Independence. In 1819, he was given command of the Asturian Battalion and sent to Cádiz on his way to fight in the colonies, but he neither he nor his men liked the idea of fighting and dying in the faraway Americas. Riego never got on the boat. Instead, on 1 January 1820, he persuaded his troops to mutiny.

Later in January, Riego proclaimed the Constitution at Las Cabezas de San Juan, between Seville and Jerez. He then commenced a tour of Andalucía, hoping to raise a following. He and his troops spent about a fortnight in Vejer, where he proclaimed the Constitution before the Council of 1814, who seem to have received his oration without comment. He did, however, succeed in relieving the town´s funds of 35000 reales to supply his horses and men. Local opinion subsequently declared this to be 'unfortunate'.

After his visit to Vejer, Riego was harassed by Vejeriego Colonel José Miranda Cabezón and his men, retreating first to Ronda and then towards Portugal, where he planned to go into exile. In mid-March, however, news arrived that the King had decided to accept the Constitution, as an option slightly preferable to outright revolution. Riego leapt into prominence, supported by ex-guerillas who had recently fought the French, demanding the implementation of the Constitution and the abolition of the Inquisition.

Elections were organised and the Cortés was convened. Riego took a leading part in the subsequent progressive government, despite being briefly imprisoned on charges of republicanism. In 1823, however, King Ferdinand dissolved parliament and began a new campaign of persecution. On 7 April 1823, in response to international concern, the French army invaded Spain. Riego resisted the invaders, as well as local absolutist groups, but was betrayed, and taken prisoner. Hundreds more were executed for speaking his name or owning his picture. He was not forgotten, however, and between 1931 and 1936, El Himno de Riego, a song written in honour of Riego, became the anthem of the Second Spanish Republic.

Fernando reigned for another ten years, while Spain, already devastated after the war, sank into decline. Bandits were everywhere, and some, like Hinojosa Cobacho, 'El Tempranillo', who was said to control most of Andalucía, had more power than the King, and a lot more respect from the people. Foreign visitors began to remark that 'Africa begins at the Pyrenees'.

Meanwhile, support for the Constitution continued to grow, and between 1823 and 1874, there was on average a rebellion somewhere every twenty months. The 1830 Revolution in France gave new impetus to the liberal movement, and in 1931, Vejer was a major focus of another liberal uprising, planned in the British-territory of Gibraltar, where Spanish law had no jurisdiction.

Cristóbal Jurado was a lawyer from Úbeda who became interested in the liberal cause and took up arms for his beliefs. In Gibraltar, he established contact with other liberal exiles Torrijos and Manzanares, and with them, planned an uprising in. In March 1831, they decided to move ahead with their plans. While Manzanares took up position in Algeciras, Jurado travelled to Vejer, from where he hoped to unite with the Cádiz branch of the movement and gather popular support. Manzanares, however, disregarded the agreed arrangements and announced the uprising in Algeciras earlier than planned, before advancing to Vejer where Jurado had assembled three hundred followers, and was now marching to Los Barrios.

On the second of March, the governor of Cádiz was assassinated by a group of conspirators in the hope of gaining popular support. However, the expected support did not materialize, the revolutionaries dithered, and the moment was lost. Believing that the revolution had succeeded in Cádiz, the insurgents declared themselves in San Fernando the same day. When they heard news of the Cádiz failure, eighty soldiers under the command of General Rosique made their way to Vejer hoping to unite with Jurado and establish contact with Manzanares, whom they believed to be in Tarifa.

On the 5th of March, Jurado proclaimed the Constitution in Vejer, while the Mayor, Diego Sevilla, trembled behind locked doors. Manzanares, meanwhile, had taken refuge in the mountains around Ronda where he was isolated from the other insurgents.

Resistance to the uprising was hastily assembled in Chiclana, and the first troops arrived in Vejer on March 6th, blockading the town against the revolutionaries' escape. Others took up positions around the town, obstructing the route to Gibraltar. Jurado was wounded while defending the pass, and concealed himself in one of the mills in Santa Lucia. Although the revolutionaries fought hard, the King's troops prevailed when more troops arrived and all the routes out of Vejer were blocked.

On the seventh of March, with no escape available, the revolutionaries had to face the possibility of surrender. The Mayor and other officials negotiated hard with the army. They had no interest in sheltering the insurgents, but on the other hand, many were native Vejeriegos, to whose families the Council would have to answer. They were also aware that the Liberal cause had many supporters in the town; the possibility of future reprisals was strong. Eventually, the Mayor agreed to give up the ringleaders on the condition that nobody was harmed.

The King's army was led by General Quesada, a man who knew his duty. He demanded unconditional surrender from the assorted insurrectionists, now garrisoned uncomfortably around the town. He asked the Mayor to consider his position overnight, and rode back down the hill. A cold, rainy night passed. The next morning, General Quesada returned. Was the Mayor ready to hand over the culprits, or did he want events to run their natural course? The Mayor held firm, preferring the responsibility for what was surely to follow to lie with the Army, rather than with himself. Later that day, the troops entered the town and rounded up four hundred men, who were promptly imprisoned. Many others managed to escape, or make themselves scarce.

Quesada, however, had received accurate intelligence about the revolt, and knew who the ringleaders were. He offered a ransom of 1000 reales for Jurado, and sat back to wait. The following day, a miller woman and her daughters arrived from Santa Lucía in a rickety cart drawn by a *burro*. The family was known locally as *'la hija de Roque'* (the Roque girls). They asked to see the general, and told him that they knew where the man he wanted was. Quesado sent a detachment of soldiers to investigate the claim, and later that day, they returned with the wounded Jurado. 'Take him away,' the General said, and the horses turned the corner towards the jail. Handing Jurado's ransom to the miller, Quesada commented 'Take it, you wicked woman, the price of your betrayal.'

The other two revolutionaries, Manzanares and Torrijos, fared little better. Manzanares was betrayed and shot in Estepona in March. Torrijos was captured and executed in Málaga several months later, following a new insurrection. By the end of the 1831, the liberal cause had been effectively repressed. A military commission was set up in Vejer with the task of passing judgment on the insurrectionists, but although several death penalties were passed, only Jurado's took effect, and many of the defendants were active in the liberal administration of 1836.

Several defendants, however, were still languishing in jail that summer, awaiting judgment; among them a young hothead called Manuel Torres, who had fought fiercely for the cause. In 1840, he would become the leader of the progressive Liberals and acquire heroic status through his determination to redistribute council land among the people of Vejer. They would later call him 'the father of the poor'. Many others escaped the law, including Captain Rosique who hid in Gibraltar, and José Berard Luque, a Cádiz merchant who turned Muslim in order to evade justice, and died in Tangiers shortly afterwards.

After receiving judgment in March 1831, Jurado asked to see a priest, and made his will. Jurado requested burial on Christian ground, and, asserting that he was free of debt, named his executors, all residents of Úbeda. Later that day, he wrote a codicil, speaking of the sadness of his position, and his loneliness as the moment of his execution grew closer. The revolution had failed and his friends had deserted him. Many of his followers had showed themselves to be cowards. At the end, wounded and vulnerable, he had been betrayed to certain death. Towards midnight, he declared that his hand was shaking too much to sign the codicil.

A few hours later, Jurado was taken to the outskirts of town, probably the cemetery of San Miguel, and executed. He was buried as requested. In later years and different times, though the people of Vejer celebrated the heroes of the Liberal insurrection, the collective sense of shame prevented them from so much as mentioning Jurado's name. The bitter final words of his will reveal his disillusion; 'Crstóbal Jurado: heroic failure.'

In September 1833, Fernando VII died and left his daughter Isabel on the throne. The succession, however, was disputed by the supporters of his brother, Don Carlos. Civil war broke out, and over the next six years, 140000 men died. Passionately devoted to the aristocracy and the church, the Carlists believed that Fernando had been soft on Liberalism, and they fought a determined guerilla campaign against the forces of progressive government. Though they never regained the throne, the Carlists caused three civil wars during the 19th century and were an important factor in the Nationalist rebellion which led to the Spanish Civil War in 1936.

One of the unintended consequences of the first Carlist war was the emergence of the anti-clericalist movement. 'Everyone in Spain follows the Church,' people said, 'one half with a candle and the other half with a club'. The rest of Europe took an interest in the war, and like the Civil War of 1936-1939, the conflict attracted foreign volunteers. One young Irish poet, Richard Chenevix Trench, pressing the family yacht into service, captured Malaga and held it briefly on behalf of the Carlists. Three decades later, he was enthroned as the Bishop of Dublin.

Meanwhile, the liberal cause was gaining momentum as its exiled supporters returned to Spain. The Queen Regent, María Christina, was obliged to collaborate with the liberals to secure the throne for her daughter, and to avoid the possibility of Carlos and his followers returning the country to an absolute monarchy. In 1834, a new Constitution was granted which extended the franchise, established a central government and guaranteed bourgeois property rights.

Two extraordinary movements now radically changed the face of Spain. From 1835 to 1837, the Ecclesiastical Confiscations of Juan Álvarez Mendizábal, who was briefly prime minister under Queen Isabel II of Spain, more often referred to simply as La Desamortización legislated for the expropriation, and privatization, of monastic properties in Spain, and most of the ancient monasteries which had been in occupation for centuries were vacated. The Mayorazgos, the entailed estates, had been in existence since 1505, when Isabel and Ferdinand had initiated them to avoid breaking up estates through inheritance by younger sons. Although property could be added to an estate, none could be sold, and the eldest son must inherit all. The 'Ley Desaviculadores' passed in 1820, revoked all entails and allowed for the sale and redistribution of previously entailed property. Locally, several seigniorial estates were broken up, the most important being the House of Medina Sidonia, but the Lobatónes, Navedas and Chirinos were also affected. The main beneficiaries were the already wealthy Marqués de Tamarón and Juan Castrillón Folquera. Financial obligations to the Dukes of Medina Sidonia finally ceased in 1878, when the charges were lifted on the last piece of communal land.

Both the Desamortisation and the disengagement from seigniorial houses caused visible changes in the appearance of the old town of Vejer. Buildings like the castle and the Casa del Mayorazgo, the home of the ducal administrator, now ceased to have a function and were gradually converted into apartments. The house of the Navedas was eventually turned into a refuge for widows. With the exception of the parish church, religious buildings also lost their function and were put to other uses, the Convento de San Francisco passing into the hands of the Ayuntamiento before becoming a shopping centre. The absence of monks and nuns in Vejer caused some difficulties for the Council, as they had previously taken much of the responsibility of caring for the sick and the poor.

During this period, Vejer's council also disposed of many of its holdings. Between 1836 and 1841, the progressive liberals, led by Manuel Torres who became Mayor in 1840, authorized the private allocation of property to landless labourers, and about a thousand country people received a piece of land. This, together with the sale of church property and municipal and seigniorial holdings, meant that around 25000 fanegas of land changed hands in 25 years, a revolution in land ownership. Most of the property that was sold, however went to the wealthy, and even those of the less wealthy who had managed to acquire some land were often obliged to sell it because they did not have the means to farm it, or to pay the taxes which attached to property ownership.

Some of the harshest effects of these developments, however, were softened by the Hazas de Suerte. Rights to the hazas had been confirmed in 1568, but by the middle of the 19th century, use of these agricultural resources was limited to the more affluent farmers, and corruption had become prevalent in allocating land. In theory, all residents were entitled to use of the hazas, but the poorest were effectively excluded because the law required them to prove that they had the capital resources to work the land. Entitlements to the hazas could be farmed on one's own account or rented out at a profit, and though the maximum allocation was officially three hazas, the big landholders habitually used their influence with the Town Council to appropriate up to twenty.

In 1840, some of the smaller farmers succeeded in regaining access to more than half the hazas, infuriating the bigger landowners. The moderate Mayor responded by retrospectively annulling the leases and returning the land to the larger landowners. To make the point absolutely clear, some of the small farmers were slapped into jail, and their property confiscated.

Although a liberal regime was now in place, this did not mean an end to conflict. Many conservatives rebranded themselves 'moderate liberals' in order to participate in the political process, and tension between them and the progressive liberals was acute. Within a few days of the new Constitution being declared, the Vejeriego liberals had established themselves as the authorities, and the young lawyer Salvador Manzorro, one of Vejer's leading liberals, became Mayor.

The moderate liberals accommodated some conservatives in their ranks and the new régime began to settle in. All went well until, in 1840, the progressive liberals made significant gains in a local election, bringing Torres into power as the Mayor. The progressive party immediately began to repair the damage done by the moderates earlier in the year, and the moderate Mayor was arrested on charges of corruption.

The moderates claimed malpractice and annulled the election, declaring another date in February. Feelings ran high, and a troop of infantry was sent to maintain order. A corrupt election was finally held in which the moderate liberals prevailed, amid accusations of betrayal and political opportunism.

In September of 1840, the national Spanish progressive party declared an objection to the Regency of Queen María Christina and a new Regent, Baldomero Espartero, was appointed. His representative in Vejer was Salvador Sánchez, who was in hiding. Sanchez was called upon to head the local Revolutionary Council, and entered the town in glory, the bells ringing and the population crowding the streets to witness his arrival. Headed by the

Vicar and sixty or seventy riders on mules and donkeys, the people of Vejer met the 'Danton of Vejer' on the Chiclana road. Sánchez, who wore an imposing hat and sported his lieutenant's stripes, was mounted on a 'majestic' horse. A military band escorted him into town.

In September 1841, portraits of the new Regent and the Queen entered Vejer in much the same style as Sánchez had done a year earlier, escorted by a military band, a troop of militia and most of the populace. A Te Deum was celebrated in the parish church and the portraits were displayed on the balconies of the Plaza de España, followed by a military procession and the distribution of bread to the people. In the evening, the band played patriotic anthems as the bells rang and fireworks exploded all around. Vejer danced till dawn.

Local conflict continued, however, and in 1842, the moderate ex-Mayor, Ildefonso Fernández Arjona was detained in the Convento of San Francisco on charges of corruption. On April the 5th of that year, the convent was set on fire by arsonists who put some burning material into a storeroom through an open window on the Calle Cerro. Arjona managed to get out, but the fire continued for five days, all but destroying the Convento. The culprits were never discovered, though accusations were made on both sides of the dispute.

The fire was a disaster for the progressive liberals, who were subsequently excluded from government by a conservative coalition specifically formed to keep them from office. On the night of January 3rd 1843, following another election annulled for malpractice, the progressive leader Sánchez Manzorro was shot at on the Plazuela, though the attack left him unharmed. Five days later, however, Antonio Castro, another progressive, was assassinated in Vejer. Alarm broke out in the town and troops were sent in once again to guarantee the conduct of the subsequent election.

A source of resentment which continued for most of the century was the scheme to drain the lake of La Janda. A concession had been granted to Don José Moret in 1822, making the company substantial landowners in their own right, but rather than carry out the work, they began to apply Rackman-esque techniques, raising rent and charging taxes on the use of the land. Some work was carried out in the early stages of the agreement, but it was inadequate - a late nineteenth century photograph shows that the lake was still there.

Rather than solving the problems caused by the latifundias, the drainage scheme added to them, raising costs and failing to produce much needed extra land for cultivation. Nevertheless, one of the consequences of the redistribution of land was the creation of an enlarged rural proletariat. By the mid-century, around 80% of the population still owned nothing, though many former liberals had converted themselves into property owners through the changes. Many of those who had rented ecclesiastical or seigniorial land had lost their homes and livelihoods.

On August the 26th 1869, at eleven o'clock in the morning, Doña María del Carmen Sanchez heard a knock on the door of her house at 8 Calle Yeseros, Vejer de la Frontera. Her husband, progressive politician Manuel Torres, the 'father of the poor' was resting and the maid was busy in the kitchen, so she answered the door herself.

Two men stood outside: Juan Ramón Mateo Garcia and Gaspar Rodriguez y Rodriguez, both Vejeriegos, and well known to her. They asked to see her husband. Carmen told them that he was resting and not available, but they were insistent, and so she called him. He came downstairs pulling on his jacket, and greeted the men politely, asking them to sit with him in the patio. They all sat, one of the visitors on each side of Manuel, and Carmen returned to the second floor of the house, leaving her husband to his business.

No sooner had she arrived on the second floor than she remembered something she had to do. It was baking day, and the maid needed a supply of flour from the locked cupboard on the first floor landing. She went back down the first flight of stairs, but before she could put the key in the lock, she heard her husband cry out loudly, 'Carmen, they are killing me!'

Carmen ran down the stairs into the patio and found Manuel doubled up in his chair with blood pouring from his side. He got up, took two steps towards her and collapsed.

Despite her shock and fear for her husband, Carmen noticed a man slipping out of the patio, whom she felt certain was one of the visitors Manuel had been entertaining a few minutes previously. She knelt down and tried to find he husband's pulse, but there was none. Manuel Torres, freedom fighter turned councillor, and twice Mayor of Vejer, was dead.

Since Carmen was able to identify the visitors, they were arrested the following day, having made no effort to conceal themselves. It should have been a short trip from the courthouse to the firing squad. But when the men were questioned, Carmen was horrified to find the case against them collapsing. The maid, who had been in the kitchen adjoining the patio when the crime was committed, was bribed to say that she had not heard the victim's shout for help, a nonsensical claim, since Carmen herself had heard it from the floor above. Her version of the time of death, therefore, could not be corroborated. Shortly afterwards, the justices ruled that she was not in full possession of her faculties after what had happened to her unfortunate husband, and that her statement was a consequence of the shock she had received.

A lengthy and expensive court case seemed imminent, but the next day, Juan Mateo confessed, explaining that he was solely responsible for the murder, Gaspar Rodriguez having left the patio before the crime was committed. Unsurprisingly, Rodriguez himself confirmed this account, and was released without further questioning.

Juan Mateo was now put in prison, and it was assumed that the case against him would be brought to a speedy and decisive resolution, but he had only been incarcerated a few hours when a groundswell of support emerged from the town's conservative contingent. Homes, businesses and officials were swiftly canvassed, and before Mateo had spent a day in jail, a large sum of money had been collected to pay for his release. He was set free shortly afterwards, and to Carmen's chagrin, took up his place in the community as if the murder had never taken place.

The widow was so deeply shocked by her husband's murder and the leniency with which the culprits had been treated that even a year afterwards, she was unable to speak of what had occurred. According to legend, she left Manuel's bloodied garments on the patio for years as a reminder to herself and others of the awful manner of his death.

This episode is representative of the state of politics in nineteenth century Andalucía, both in the strength of feeling apparently expressed, but also in its serpentine entanglement of the personal and political. Although many conservative politicians loathed Manuel Torres and everything he stood for, and if not actually prepared to slaughter him themselves, were more than willing to forgive and support those who did, the murder was not entirely political. The two assassins, in fact, had been slighted by Torres over the matter of a will, and the murder was little more than an expression of spite, financially motivated rather than politically.

In the overheated context of local affairs, however, it was easy to use politics as a smokescreen for murder, especially when, like Juan Mateo, the criminal was a cousin of the current, conservative Mayor. The assassination of Torres marked the end of liberal support among the disillusioned rural poor. From now on, they would turn to anarchism or socialism to fulfil their aspirations.

In 1868, resentment against the corrupt and promiscuous Queen Isabel II and her family came to a head, and she was deposed in what at the time was called 'The Glorious Revolution'. A substitute, Prince Amadeo from Italy, was recruited, partly on account of his liberal views. Amadeo, however, was resented by the Spanish, and after two years, he thankfully abdicated. The resulting power vacuum was filled by the First Republic, which lasted eleven months and in that time managed to get through four leaders. At the end of 1874, Isabel's son, Alfonso XII, was proclaimed king.

The episode polarized political attitudes, and many 'moderates' now declared themselves outright conservatives, represented in Vejer by the Marqués of Tamarón and his family, the Moras. Among progressive liberals, loyalties were fragmented, and while the monarchist progressives were supported by the wealthy Shelly and Castrillón families, republicans gained a following among ordinary people.

Meanwhile, the anarchists, organized into worker's unions, were secretly growing in strength. Both they and the federal republicans favoured social change through revolution, while the more mainstream factions inclined towards peaceful methods. In October 1872, there had been an Andalucían uprising in favour of a federal republic. On December 8th, the same year, the revolutionaries had their day. In the early morning, anarchists from Paterna began to gather in Vejer, ready to conduct a propaganda campaign. Their fiery spirit readily communicated itself to the working people in the town and at ten o'clock on the morning, when a member of the Guardia Civil fired on a demonstrator in San Miguel, wounding him slightly, the trouble began. Led by republicans and anarchists, the crowd came out onto the street, shouting 'viva la República Federal!' and marched on the Town Hall, demanding to see the Secretary. When he did not appear, they smashed the furniture and hauled the archives out onto the Plaza de España, where they burned every last paper. The Munipal Archive, containing records dating back to the middle ages was completely destroyed.

The rioters then raided the municipal treasury and took possession of its funds, after which they demanded that the church bells be rung. Still shouting for a republic, they went off to La Barca in search of the town archivist, Franciso Chica, whom they stabbed to death, believing him to be responsible for corruption. Two or three other Vejeriegos were also wounded in the course of the day's events, including the chief of the Guardia Municipal. There is a story that sometime during the day, the insurgents held a political meeting in the churchyard to give a Christian burial to a fallen comrade, Guillén, though this is not documented.

Realising that retribution would not be long in coming, the insurrectionists requisitioned enough horses and supplies to equip two hundred people, and forty or fifty armed revolutionaries forced themselves into the houses of prominent citizens, including the Shellys and the Castrillóns, collecting large sums of money which were handed over in order to avoid even worse evils.

The insurgents left Vejer under cover of darkness, but the following morning at dawn, they reappeared in Medina Sidonia, ready for a re-run of the previous day. The town, however, had been alerted by telegraph, and the attempt failed. The culprits were seized and transported to Cuba or the

Phillipines, from whence none returned, and Vejer was reprimanded by the provincial government for its ineffectual treatment of the uprising. The repentant Mayor resigned and José Nuñez was appointed in his place.

After so much unrest, it is hardly surprising that with the Restoration of Alfonso XII in 1874, the Army took charge of the nation's affairs, presiding over an increasingly corrupt political system. In 1886, the results of the general election were mistakenly published the day before voting began. Many leaders were little more than dictators: when asked on his deathbed if he forgave his enemies, Prime Minister Navaez replied, 'I don't have any enemies, Father, I have shot them all.'

Not every enemy carried firearms. Dangerous diseases like smallpox were being brought under control by vaccination, though there were epidemics in 1873, and 1879. An early 19th century epidemic, which killed 7000 in Cádiz and 10000 in Jerez, completely missed Vejer, as did malaria, possibly because the town was too high and the winds were too strong. Quarantine regulations prevented the spread of cholera into the town in 1890- 91, but a previous epidemic in 1834 had caused many deaths and wiped out entire families.

By the end of the nineteenth century, the ancient Hospital of San Juan was in a very poor state, though in 1877, a benefits committee set up by the council had chanelled some money its way. After 1880, more land was put under cultivation and agricultural output increased. The demand for labour grew and Vejer's population increased to 8000 inhabitants. Vejeriegos lost interest in politics after the Restoration because the system was so clearly rigged that it was a waste of time participating.

After the 1860s, Liberal and anticlerical sentiments were a feature of the Freemasons, a movement which was represented in Vejer by three lodges, the Fe y Esperanza, the Turdetania, and the Caridad. Each of these represented different aspects of liberal thought, and all were significant in forming the social and political context of the time. Between 1868 and 1898, Masonic presidents were in power for around half the time.

As the 19th century ended, a deceptive calm prevailed, but the rifts in Spanish society remained. The peace was not to last.

Chapter 13

Vejer
The Twentieth Century

Francisco Franco, dictator of Spain

Antonio Morillo Crespo, crusading Mayor of Vejer

!UPTHEREPUBLIC!
Samuel Beckett

It's tempting to divide twentieth century Spain into three periods: Pre Franco, Franco, and Post Franco. Naturally, the divisions are not really quite so clear. Within the Franco era, for example, there were large differences between the brutal forties and the more affluent sixties, when money from the USA poured into the Spanish economy in exchange for the right to build military bases on Spanish soil.

The Spanish twentieth century effectively began in 1898 when Spain lost the last colony, Cuba, to the USA, undermining the government's credibility and seriously weakening its political system. Spain's failure in the Rif War (1920) had a similar effect. At the start of the twentieth century, Andalucía remained undeveloped, with many of its citizens experiencing hardship, and its land only producing 70 percent of what was achieved in other provinces. Antiquated agricultural methods brought poor harvests, and fifty percent of the braceros, or landless classes, were illiterate.

The hated Guardia Civil kept Andalucía in order, and in the poverty stricken pueblos, emigration to one of the large cities, or to other countries, often seemed the only hope of advancement, a trend that would continue during the twentieth century. Class hatred and rural discontent contributed to the growing success of the Anarchists in the region. Although in Vejer itself the population rose, much of the increase was due to Barbate's economic expansion. A substantial flow of immigrants had arrived, attracted by the tunafishing and associated industries. The population was spread among many outlying hamlets and farming communities, though the city of Vejer was by far the largest, housing more than half the population and possessing 704 buildings. The next in size was Barbate with 118.

Although the end of the Old Regime in the previous century had signified the end of feudal society and the privileges of the nobility and the Church, the continuing unequal distribution of wealth is clearly apparent in the Vejer's land registries of 1854 and 1906. In 1874, the main landowners were the Lobatones, the Moras, the Castrillóns, the Navedas, and as always, the Dukes of Medina Sidonia. In 1906, it is the Castrillóns, the Moras, and the fabulously rich Gabriel Ponce de Leon Alba. The Dukes of Medina Sidonia have morphed into their offshoots the Marquesses of Martorell and San Felices of Aragon.

The number of individuals paying land taxes has dropped from 1715 to 1005 individuals, a clear sign that land was now concentrated in fewer hands, and the number of people benefitting from the redistribution had shrank from 1000 to 500 by 1906. The poorest, meanwhile, the braceros and jornaleros, were constantly in want and frequently obliged to ask from assistance from the parish. In addition, there were always three or four hundred beggars or severely impoverished people who were obliged to live more or less permanently on charity.

In 1900, agriculture was still the principal industry. Wheat was the main crop, occupying half the available land, followed by vines, olives and fruit trees, though the production of oranges had declined since the middle of the nineteenth century. 37% of agricultural land was used for grazing. There was some woodland on the hillsides of La Breña, producing wild olives, used for making agricultural implements, cork and pine. Vejer exported cereals, cork, oranges and cattle, and imported oil and wine; 80 litres a year for every inhabitant.

At the end of the 19th century, largely because of wheat sales, Vejer was in surplus, though little of the profit ended up in the pockets of the workers. Agricultural labourers lived in unremitting poverty, and were absolutely at the mercy of their wealthy employers. Labourers worked an average of

250 days a year, though this was not guaranteed, and job security was unheard of. At the end of the nineteenth century, a kilo of bread cost two reales, a litre of wine 1.5, and a kilo of meat almost two pesetas or eight reales. The wage of an unskilled worker varied between five and seven reales a day, though at harvest time they might get eleven. A mule train attendant earned 1.75 pesetas a day, or 1.25 for accompanying a donkey. A real was a quarter of a peseta, worth a gramme of silver; a day was de sol a sol -twelve hours. There was no housing provision and labourers had to supply their own tools, but unusually for Spain, Andalucían women rarely worked in the fields.

The fishing industry in Barbate produced sardines and mackerel as well as tuna, in the traditional *almabraba,* the line fishing industry. After the Dukes of Medina Sidonia lost their privileges in 1817, the fishermen themselves were entitled to run the fisheries, but it wasn't long before the local aristocracy got in on the act. In 1822, the Marquis of Villafranca took over control, on the understanding that he continued to use the traditional line fishing technique, rather than industrial fishing techniques such as the use of the trawl net.

Control of the fisheries remained in his hands for about 40 years until in 1880, the concession passed to Serafín Romeu, and subsequently to his son of the same name. This family was largely responsible for the expansion of the town in the late nineteenth century. Profits leapt from 1500 pesetas in 1876 to 2 million in 1920, and Romeu junior was offered a knighthood for his achievements. He first proposed that he should take the title Count of Vejer, but this idea was firmly rejected, and he had to settle for Barbate instead.

After the seigniorial collapse, the social structure gradually began to change. Trades guilds, which had controlled working conditions for craftsmen, gradually disappeared and craftsmen were allowed to trade freely, though the system of apprenticing young men to master craftsmen persisted. In Vejer, the carpenters', shoemakers' and barbers' guilds survived until the 1930s; the shoemakers were so well organized that they had their own band of musicians for fiestas and parades. The social and philanthropic aspects of the guilds were missed, however, and in 1910, master carpenter

Manuel Muñoz Rodriguez founded 'The United Guilds' for the mutual support of all workers. This union merged with the National General workers' union in the 2nd republic and was suppressed under Franco.

Until the start of the twentieth century, Vejer's infrastructure, as everywhere in Andalucia, was of the strictly traditional type. Drinking water had to be purchased or hauled up the hill from the well at La Barca, one good reason for keeping a donkey on the patio. Aljibes, rainwater storage chambers under the patios, were a useful source of water for plants and animals and for washing clothes, but not everybody had access to them. There was no domestic electricity supply, and street lighting was supplied by petrol lanterns on the main streets. Of toilet arrangements, it is better not to speak. Hygiene left much to be desired; most roads were not paved, and filthy water ran down the centre of many, collecting in odorous pools. Cesspools were conveniently placed in front of houses, constituting a health hazard.

In 1904, however, owing to a stroke of genius on the part of a local aristocrat, Vejer became one of the first towns in Andalucía to acquire running water and electricity. The Count of Villariezo, one of the heirs of the Dukes of Medina Sidonia, who owned the springs at Santa Lucía, established a company to supply light and water to Vejer, and in 1906, electric lights blazed out in Vejer for the first time (though only in the best houses), and running water arrived on the hilltop, pumped to a store in El Santo, from where it was distributed, also to a select group of private subscribers. For once, a local aristocrat was giving something to the town instead of taking from it; as Antonio Muñoz Rodriguez wryly comments, 'noblesse oblige'. For many years, the headquarters of the company were situated on the Corredera, next to the open-air cinema, now a car park.

In 1949, the municipal council took over the water supply, and created a public fountain on the Plaza de España, but the company continued to supply water from the springs in Santa Lucia, until the Municipality bought it in 1978. A new pumping station was built, popularly known 'la fabrica', which brought welcome employment to the town.

Social infrastructure was also beginning to show its age as the twentieth century began. There had been a Hospital of Mercy next to the Church of

San Juan since the 15th century, but it relied largely on the religious order for funding, and after the desamortisation, its income was greatly reduced, with the result that it closed in 1891.

Though by 1900, dangerous diseases like smallpox and yellow fever were being brought under control by vaccination, the 'flu pandemic of 1918, took the local authorities by surprise. The 'flu, which killed between 50 and 100 million people (compared with 16 million who died as a result of the war) was probably the cause of more deaths than the plague; its spread was assisted by the constant movements of troops to and from the battlefield. The disease was known as the 'Spanish flu', not because it originated in Spain, but because King Alfonso XIII, who had worked with prisoners of war, was its most famous victim. As Spain was neutral in the 1914-18 war, and thus did not impose wartime censorship, his illness was the most widely publicised.

As soon as the danger was understood, the council took all possible precautions, Vejer schools were closed, entrance to the town was controlled, public buildings disinfected, and quinine handed out to the victims to lower the fever. Nevertheless, there were many victims. During the month in which the outbreak lasted, around 260,000 Spaniards died of influenza; in Spain, the epidemic was called 'the French 'flu'.

Because many of its population lived in remote areas, Vejer's literacy rates were among the worst in the province. Despite the existence of seven primary schools, only 14.6% of the men and 11.3% of the women could read, compared with 35.8% and 27.4% in the province as a whole. In all probability, even fewer could write. This was not, of course, because young Vejeriegos were less educable than others, but because there was no educational provision in the country districts. Even when families owned houses in the town, these were often only used for special occasions like the feria, or times when medical attention or a midwife was required. Too often, educational provision was left to dedicated individuals who were prepared to give their time and effort to this cause. One such individual was Francisco Metola – Padre Jandillo- who made superhuman efforts to bring education to country children, aided and supported by the Sisters of Mercy.

In other areas, few changes had been made to the town's transport infrastructure, though a new road to Medina Sidonia had opened in 1894 after 20 years of rather less than intensive building activity. Other roads were in a woeful state, unevenly surfaced and clogged by animals and pedestrians. Many amounted to no more than mule tracks. One of the casualties of the early twentieth century was the port at La Barca. As there was no customs point at the port, traders were obliged to travel to San Fernando to do their paperwork, an expensive and time-consuming nuisance. By the time this was put right, it was too late. Traffic moved to the roads and the old port closed down in the nineteen twenties after centuries of service to the town and its people.

A coup in 1923, which brought a right-wing dictatorship to Spain, took everybody by surprise except the King, who had agreed to it. Miguel Primo de Rivera, the Marquis of Estella, Spain's new and more or less self-appointed leader, was born in Jerez de la Frontera in 1870, an old-fashioned country squire with a military background, part of what Gerald Brenan called 'a hard-drinking, whoring, horse-loving aristocracy'. He had served in Cuba and the Philippines, before joining the Ministry of War. Later, he travelled in Northern Europe and was promoted to Brigadier-General after a campaign in Morocco. Frustrated by the government's inability to deal with the problems of the age, in 1923, he headed a military coup and was appointed Prime Minister by the King. Rivera suspended the Constitution and ruled as a dictator.

Rivero's military dictatorship emerged under the pretext of eliminating corruption and rescuing the country from professional politicians. Soon after the coup, his people descended on the smaller towns and rigorous inspections were made, which invariably resulted in punishment all round. Rivera's regime abolished political parties, dissolved the Cortés, and placed the Ayuntimientos under military control. The secretary of Vejer's Ayuntimiento became one of the first victims of the regime when, after visiting the parish priest to express his concerns, he was shot in his office at the town hall.

On the first of October 1923, Captain José Tristán and his men arrived in Vejer to appoint a new Mayor and council, and rapidly placed the previous Mayor and several officials under arrest. A new Ayuntimiento was appointed at the end of 1923, representing Rivera's new Patriotic Union party, and Rivera visited Vejer to open the party headquarters on Calle Juan Bueno. He came back again in June 1925 to preside over the blessing of their new flag.

Apart from the occasional, though regrettable shooting, Vejer did not suffer too badly under the Rivera regime. The new council, headed by Jaime Mora Figueroa, changed the road signs, cleaned up the administration and initiated some important public works, including the removal of the slaughterhouse to San Miguel and the construction of a market in its place. They created the first municipal library and improved the local roads. Nobody liked living under a dictator, however, and when Rivera's exploits became ludicrous, the King shunted him off into exile, and the town administration changed again. The new council, of course, repudiated everything that had been done by the previous one, and changed the road signs back to what they had been before. They also went back to their old ways. In 1931, the second Republic was proclaimed, and the council was suspended for corruption.

The left, republicans, anarchists and socialists, expected a lot from the Republic, but although there were many important reforms nationally - the number of children in secondary education was increased from 20000 to 70000 - in Andalucía, the radical changes needed did not occur. Agrarian reform was feeble, and strongly opposed by the great landowners.

The social system was explosive, with millions of hectares of land divided between a few landowners, while the vast majority of people had nothing, and though wages had increased since the beginning of the century, they

1936—the triumph of the Popular Front celebrated in the Plaza de España

were still lower than elsewhere, despite the fact that Andalucían workers were as productive as others in Spain. Moreover, Andalucían workers, with a history of anarchism reaching back to the previous century, were increasingly politicised. 'La tierra para el que la trabaja' (the land for those who work on it) was a popular saying in the area.

Municipal elections were held immediately, and the Constitution was restored. However, the vindictive implementation of the anti-clerical Article 26 caused violent resentment among members of the Catholic Church and its supporters. Writer Miguel de Unamuno observed that 'Here in Spain, we are all Catholics, even the atheists.' A gap opened up in the electorate which seemed irreparable.

Nevertheless, the following two years were remarkable for a range of social reforms; freedom of speech and freedom of association, suffrage extended to women, and divorce. The nobility was stripped of its special legal status. Most of these reforms, however, were removed in 1933, when the general election was won by right-wing groups. The following two years were called 'the black years' as the effects of the Depression began to make themselves felt. Mining towns exploded in murderous rebellion, and troops were sent in. In 1936, new elections were called, and the different left-wing groups united in the famous 'Popular Front', which was elected into power on February 16th.

Revolutionary sentiments were sometimes expressed in violent revolts, which were brutally suppressed by the authorities. In 1933, at Benalup-Casas Viejas, a few kilometres to the north of Vejer, anarchists overthrew

Guardia de Asalto , Benalup 1933

the local authorities and took over the town hall, flying the red and black flag from the Ayuntimiento. Nobody was killed in the uprising, despite a substantial population of wealthy families.

The Civil Guard sent to Medina Sidonia for help, and a detachment of Guardia de Asalto, (assault guards) arrived to deal with the revolt. Most of the anarchists left, and created a new base outside the town, but one veteran anarchist, Seisdedos, (six fingers), barricaded himself into his house with his family and refused to open his door. When force was attempted, he fired on the Guardia, killing two of them – his daughter-in-law Josepha acted as gun-loader. The Guardia attacked with machine guns, but still Seisdedos would not surrender. During the night, firing stopped, and two of his family escaped. One of them, Libertaria, survived until 1936, only to be murdered by Nationalists on the road to Medina Sidonia.

The following morning, the soldiers, furious at being thwarted, surrounded the house with petrol and burned it down, killing all the occupants. Soldiers and police then arrested anyone in the village who possessed a gun, marched them to the smoking ashes of the cottage and their dead colleagues, and shot them in the back. Captain Rojas of the Guardia later admitted that they had dealt cruelly with the militants, even shooting people who were just looking out of their windows.

Rojas was sentenced to twenty one years' imprisonment for his part in the incident, which provoked outrage throughout Spain, and almost certainly brought down the government in the municipal elections which followed shortly afterwards. The incident was a spectacular own goal for the republican government, creating enough bad publicity to wipe out the good effects of its social reforms, and resulting in the election of a near-fascist regime which certainly did not have the interests of the people at heart.

Elections were called for Nov 19th, and in Vejer, where the memory of Benalup was still fresh, the atmosphere was charged with violence. A political meeting was arranged, and the people gathered on the Patio San Francisco to hear the different parties present their parts of view, but when the right wing group started to expound on 'The Cross and the Sword' they were laughed off the podium, and had to retreat to the Casa Tamarón for sanctuary, followed by the jeering crowd, who spent the entire evening mocking and catcalling at them through the windows.

Mockery or not, since the anarchists abstained from the elections, the right-wing CEDA had the victory. The new government restored the Catholic Church to its former position of influence and sidelined the agrarian reform so important to Andalucía. Seizing their opportunity, employers throughout Spain tried to raise rents and lower wages, and in reaction, anarchist action intensified. The Seville-Barcelona train was derailed, shootings multiplied and strikes broke out in different areas, some lasting for weeks. Serious rebellions took place, notably at Saragossa, where Buenaventura Derruti and his revolutionary committee fought police and the army for several days. Militancy increased everywhere, bringing women out onto the streets for the first time, singing and dancing in groups.

Everywhere, too, political opinion was polarized, and as the months went by, Spain looked more and more like a nation at war. In 1934, the Socialists landed several cases of weapons in Asturias, alarming government and people alike. In October of the same year, workers' alliances rebelled In January 1936, Prime Minister Manuel Azana arranged an electoral coalition and pact to be signed by various left-wing political organisations for the purpose of contesting the election; the Frente Popular (Popular Front) included the Spanish Socialist Workers' Party (PSOE), Communist Party of Spain (PCE), the Workers' Party of Marxist Unification (POUM), Republican Left (IR) and Republican Union Party (UR). The coalition was supported by Galician and Catalan nationalists, the socialist Workers' General Union (UGT), and the anarchist trade union, the Confederación Nacional del Trabajo (CNT). Many anarchists, however, preferred abstention. The right, meanwhile, organised their own coalition, which they named the National Front.

The election was called for February 1936, and resulted in a narrow victory for the Popular Front. When the results were declared, there was rejoicing in the Plaza de España, as there was all over Spain. It seemed that at last Spain might become a stable democratic republic, with all the benefits that implied for Andalucía's downtrodden poor. True to its word, however, the National Front did not accept the results of the election, and even before they were published, General Francisco Franco and others were recommending an immediate coup d'etat.

The victorious National Front were not shy about acknowledging their victory, and the atmosphere in Vejer was triumphalist. Left-wingers taunted their defeated opponents, intimidated them with knives and ostentatiously made revolutionary salutes. The streets rang to the sound of the Internationale, infuriating 'people of means' and the nucleus of working people who had supported the National Front.

One of the most influential right-wing groups was the Falange, headed by Jose Antonio Primo de Rivera, the son of the former dictator. The Falange was a fascist group inspired by the Italian dictator Mussolini. They had a substantial following in Vejer, as in most places, but after the victory of the Popular Front, their existence was precarious. On the 14th of April, twenty six members of the Falange were arrested for no particular reason and imprisoned in Chiclana. Ten days later, however, they were mysteriously released without charge.

The confrontational attitude was not entirely gratuitous. Nobody expected the political right to accept the new order without a struggle, and it came as no surprise when, after a string of violent incidents, a group of Army colonels stationed in Morocco planned a coup d'état for the 17th of July. The plotters signalled the beginning of the coup by broadcasting the code phrase, 'Over all of Spain, the sky is clear'. Several Spanish cities, including Cádiz, immediately declared their allegiance to the rebels, and Cádiz was subsequently an important disembarkation point for incoming troops.

The Spanish Civil War had begun, though nobody in Spain used that name

Republican wreckage of the parish church.

for the conflict. To the Carlists, it was the Fourth Carlist War. The Nationalists called it 'the Crusade', emphasizing their perception that this was a religious war. To the Republicans, it was 'The rebellion'.

The coastal towns near Cádiz were immediately aware of the Nationalist invasion, and tension rose. During the 18th of July, representatives of the Republican groups came and went in Vejer, giving instructions for acquiring guns and distributing them among the population. At eleven in the evening the exhausted and overwrought workers met with their different organizations and celebrated the day's activities with a glass or two of wine. At one in the morning, re-invigorated and fired with righteous indignation, they decided to investigate the rumour that a cache of Nationalist arms was concealed in the Hospital de la Merced.

At the hospital, they evacuated the occupants, who struggled away as best they could in search of shelter. The hospital was locked and barricaded and the search began. By five in the morning, however, no weapons had been found, and the searchers decided that they must be concealed in the chapel. At five thirty, when the priest turned up for Mass, the chapel was also searched, also without any result, At half past six, the infuriated workers arrested four priests and locked them up in the municipal jail on Calle La Fuente, but the elusive weapons still did not appear and the priests steadfastly denied their existence.

The following day, labourers flooded into the town armed with cudgels and stones, ready to defend the Republic with all the means at their disposal. The town became a pressure-cooker, seething with rage and resounding to threats of defiance. Anti-clerical feelings ran high and the suspicion persisted that the Church was somehow concealing arms. At eleven o'clock at night, the crowd made their way to the church where they forced an entry and launched themselves into an orgy of destruction, reducing the interior to a state of waste. The crowd tore apart clerical vestments, spitting and and urinating on them, and opened the tombs of the Lobatónes and other wealthy families, scattering the remains about. Piles of images, altarpieces, candelabras, chalices and other ecclesiastical items were heaped in the doorway and rolled about in the street as bystanders shouted encouragement. The Rosario church was given the same treatment. By five o'clock the following morning, the wreck was total and not an altar in town was left standing. As one participant remarked, 'it's been a busy night.'

Gradually, the frenzy subsided and the National Confederation of Labour, hoping to create a diversion, called a meeting on the Plaza de España. The crowd gathered, still angry, and ready to begin an assault on the houses of the wealthy, but after a night's exertion on the churches, they were drained. The speaker's calming words took effect and they began to trudge home, all passion spent.

They had no time to get home, however, because the news arrived that a lorry load of Nationalist soldiers was approaching. The crowd fled in all directions, and the lorry began its laborious ascent up the winding and narrow road into town. Half way up, the approach was blocked by a fallen (or pushed) tree. The lorry reversed back down the hill and took the Barbate road, from where they entered the town via San Miguel.

By the time they had arrived on the northern outskirts of town, a group of militants was waiting. They opened fire on the soldiers, wounding four of them, but the soldiers fought back and killed several of the militants. They then drove directly to the headquarters of the Civil Guard, who promptly signed up for the Nationalist side, except for the Captain, whom the Republicans had already put in jail. At 12.30, the priests were set free. Later that afternoon, when peace was restored, members of the Falange and the Civil Guard toured the town, shouting 'Viva España!' to encourage those who had been alarmed by the events of the previous two days.

Retribution came swiftly. Between fifty and eighty people were summarily executed. The Mayor, a peaceable individual, was shot apparently just because he was there to be shot, and as the conflict escalated, it was used as a cover for terror tactics, and also acts of personal revenge. Of the ones who were left alive, many were seized by panic and slank off, to spend the next three decades in submission to their feudal overlords.

The area was therefore rapidly subdued, lacking the size, power or equipment to resist. Both Nationalist and Republican armies kidnapped young men to fight on one side or the other and carried them, disorientated, to other parts of Spain. One local family lost four sons in this way.

As the months went by, however, undercover resistance gathered force. Efforts were made to undermine the Republican order in the coastal towns, and although these never succeeded in destabilising the regime, the provided an annoying distraction and diverted resources. The guerillas in the hills were supported by 'enlaces' (links) in urban areas, some of them female relatives of the fighters. Many of these brave people lost their lives, but others were supported by the rural communities, who kept them concealed, often for months or years. One local resident recalls that her uncles learned to read only because their parents gave sanctuary to a Republican fighter who also happened to be a teacher.

After 1940, Vejer was occupied by Moroccan troops, whose prominence, exotic in their turbans and sandals, caused a German photographer, Wilhelm Kukas Kristle, to entitle a photograph taken in 1943 'This is not Morocco, it is the south of Spain, Vejer de la Frontera de Cádiz.' Though few Vejeriegos remember the 'moros' personally, their presence has entered into the collective memory of the town, and they are remembered as one of the most striking features of the post civil war years.

'We kept the Barbary pirates out for five hundred years,' one Vejeriega told me, 'and there they were, by consent of the Government.' The resentment has scarcely subsided yet.

Initially, however, the coup was unsuccessful and the government retained control of most of the country. The revolutionaries then began a military campaign to bring the rest of Spain under control. While the Republicans were supported by Russia, Hitler's Germany provided assistance to the Nationalist side. Neither France nor Britain was prepared to intervene on behalf of Spain's democratically elected Republican government, though the argument over intervention brought down the French government, but approximately 35000 volunteers fought in the International Brigades, suffering around 18000 casualties. More than 4000 of these came from Britain, Ireland and the Commonwealth, of whom over 500 were killed. Many were members of the Communist Party, and recent research suggests that perhaps 20% were Jewish in origin. The volunteers came from working class backgrounds, and industrial occupations, with large numbers from the South Wales valleys and the large industrial cities. The average age for the volunteers from Britain was twenty-nine.

The war lasted for three years, until, in the early months of 1939, Barcelona, Madrid and Valencia were taken. The British government did not wait for the final outcome, but recognised the Franco regime on February 27th, a month before Madrid became Nationalist. On March 31st, Spain's new Fascist government signed a five year friendship pact with Nazi Germany. The British refused an urgent request to help Republican refugees, and thousands finally died in German concentration camps. Others fought for the French resistance during the Second World War.

The Civil War claimed 800,000 lives, split families and rendered much of Spain's agricultural land unusable for years. More than 50,000 Spaniards emigrated permanently to South America. By 1942, two million individuals had passed through the Spanish jails for crimes against the regime, and an estimated 150,000 people were executed.

It is lucky that Vejer's beautiful church survived the conflict. The assault in 1936 was only one of 4,850 similar acts of destruction carried out during the war; 150 churches were completely destroyed and another 1.850 were reduced almost to ruins. Six thousand priests were executed, including thirteen bishops, as the Republicans exorcised their rage against the conservative Catholic Church.

Unlike some other nations, the Spanish people never accepted Fascism, but fought against it with their last ounce of strength. In the aftermath, the Spanish did not talk about it much – the scars were too deep. An amnesty was signed in 1977, exonerating members of the Franco regime for all crimes of a political nature, though in recent years, the United Nations committee for Human Rights has advised that the amnesty should now be lifted. Despite the efforts of crusading judge Balthazar Garvin, this request has not been met.

To most other Europeans, the issues surrounding the Civil War are clear. Having fought, and won, a decisive war against Fascism, we regard the Franco era as self-.evidently evil and asume that the Spanish think the same. Many do, of course, but some members of the older generation mourn an age when morality was clear and conservative values were upheld.

After the war was over, the new regime configured itself as a civil and military dictatorship, and Francisco Franco 'the sphinx without a secret' took control of the government. Rights of free speech and free association were cancelled, as were most other civil rights. Franco's regime existed in two distinct phases: the 'famine' from 1939 to 1949, when food and other commodities were scarce, partly as the result of a series of terrible droughts, and the rest, when things weren't quite so bad.

The early phase of Franco's regime is etched on the hearts of those who suffered it. Rationing, and its inevitable evil twin, the black market, dominated the economy, and the constant presence of the army in the form of 'los moros' caused untold resentment. Small boys were put into uniforms and marched up and down the Corredera to prepare them for a Nationalist future, and real soldiers goose-stepped around the Plaza de España, making a great display of their bayonets. The Falange took over local government and kept their headquarters near the Ayuntamiento building. Spain was isolated from the rest of Europe and suffered a trade blockade. Meanwhile, the people starved in appalling poverty and had no remedy in the face of Franco's brutal repression.

Finally, the Cold War came to Spain's rescue. In 1953, Spain and the United States signed the Pact of Madrid, which gave Spain financial assistance in return for hosting American military bases. Food and powdered milk, as well as clothes, were distributed among the neediest, and by 1955, the economy had returned to pre-Civil War levels. Vejer now saw a huge expansion in public works, promoted by the Ayuntamiento and financed by the economic expansion. The Corredera, Plaza de España and, Mercado de Abastos were improved, taking on their present forms, streets were paved and cobbled and running water was installed in every house.

At the end of the 1950s, the International Monetary Fund encouraged the creation of a series of economic development plans which marked the start of the Desarollo, the Spanish economic miracle. New industries sprang up all over Spain and suddenly, the streets and squares were empty as people began to emigrate to the big cities, or to other European countries. Spain became the ninth largest economy in the world, with a growth rate second only to Japan's. In Vejer, new schools and roads were built and new homes sprang up in the San Miguel and Buenavista areas, forming the nucleus of the new town.

After the death of Franco in November 1975, Spain became a democracy, with a new constitution. As restrictions on freedom of expression were lifted, a cultural renaissance occurred and artists like Pedro Almódavar and Antonio Banderas came to prominence. Vejer's infrastructure was strengthened, with several important projects including the construction of the a new road around the outskirts of the town, a care home for the elderly and a new health centre, replacing the one which had previously existed on the Corredera. A sports centre was constructed in San Miguel and an industrial estate appeared near Santa Lucia, all helping to improve the lives of Vejeriegos of every age. After Spain joined the EEC (now the European Union) in 1986, the national infrastructure was improved and Spain became prosperous.

One of the most important and significant projects undertaken in Vejer since the 1970s has been the restoration of the ancient walls and buildings of the old town, driven by the innovative and crusading mayor, Antonio Morillo Crespo. The work was not complete until the end of the 1990s, but some of the prettiest corners of Vejer are the result of this era, as the jigsaw of the old town was patiently fitted together and creativity united with perseverance and careful research.

Not everybody viewed the proceedings in such a positive light. Some houses near the old walls were made the subject of compulsory purchase orders and demolished, their owners obliged to move to the new town. Any property which contained an ancient feature might attract the interest of the restorers and Vejeriegos who found interesting items during the process of renovating their houses became adept at covering them up and saying nothing rather than face potential disruption.

Tourism first became a reality in Vejer in the nineteen sixties. Since then, the trickle has increased, if not to a flood, certainly to a steady stream, and has occasioned the opening of some excellent hotels and restaurants.

Nevertheless, in the year 2000, provision for tourism was limited compared with what it is today. James Stuart's photograph perfectly illustrates the mood of a village in transition. In the early years of the 21st century, he would go on to found the Casa del Califa hotel, one of the defining locations of Vejer's tourist scene. But in 1988, he was still just a guy with a Beetle and a surfboard in a sleepy hilltop town where mules provided transport and all the houses were white.

Chapter 14

Costa de la Luz

Vejer has kept its typically Andalucían character: small patios, narrow streets and whitewashed facades where you can stroll, and mix with its people, fiestas, customs and general friendliness. Get to know Vejer!
- Vejer de la Frontera: tourist Guide

As the twenty first century progresses, tourism seems more and more the lifeblood of the town, and as this edition goes to press , Vejer is acquiring a reputation as a 'gastro-village'. In 2013, Vejer was named 'the second prettiest village in Spain' and in January 2014 became part of the network 'the prettiest villages in Spain'.

Prettiness is only acquired at a price, but it is a price that the town in general has been prepared to pay. Enhanced and dignified by the renovation of its ancient walls, Vejer de la Frontera entered the twenty first century as a place of extraordinary beauty and charm and a year or so later, the present writer saw it and decided to stay. This was not an isolated event. As some of the local people moved out to the new town in San Miguel, foreigners, mainly Germans and the British, moved in, and Vejer now has a substantial expatriate community, extending into the country areas of La Muela and San Ambrosio.

An associated problem, however, lies with the many second homes and properties dedicated to holiday letting in the high season. While many of these properties are well-maintained, some are not and a changing progression of fortnightly visitors is not the same as a neighbour. Plants are not always looked after, dust collects and some of the heart goes out of the community. It cannot be denied that housing in the old town as not as affordable as it is in the new. Some older Vejeriegos look back nostalgically to a time when the town was quieter, more intimate, and when everybody knew everybody else.

Defenders of the part-time community argue that many of these houses were rescued from neglect and decay and that young Vejeriegos could not have afforded the capital outlay needed to restore them. It is also true that traditionally, Vejeriegos often left their houses empty for long periods while they pursued their occupations in the country. Nevertheless, one cannot have too many empty houses in a community without sacrificing some of its vitality.

At the start of the twenty first century, the old town of Vejer possessed 734 homes, 41 of which were empty and 175 - about a quarter- were second homes kept by people from the country or outside the area. Building regulations in Vejer limit the height of buildings within the walled enclosure and most of these houses are built on two or three storeys, with their original pitched roofs intact, though some have been replaced by terraces. Most of these houses were built between the 17th and 19th centuries.

The age of the houses and the narrowness of the streets create problems of infrastructure and emergency access. Compromises have been found: the police ride motorcycles and dump trucks are used for moving building materials. In general, the town is well-lit and well preserved, though some unsuitable additions have been made; plastic or aluminium windows, wrought iron gates and ugly modern doors. Disabled access is an ongoing problem, which has been creatively and effectively solved in most of the major buildings.

As the years go by, Vejer's economic hopes are increasingly focused on tourism. This is understandable in the context of rural Andalucía, where farmers struggle to compete with cheap imports, sometimes from developing nations which can barely manage to feed themselves.

Tourism, however, is a hard and unpredictable master, which places a town's prosperity at the mercy of outsiders. There will be little point in building a new hotel on the coast if it empties beds in the town, and the recent development at La Noria, still with many empty houses, shows how the best-laid plans can go awrey. The jobs tourism creates are often temporary and badly-paid, and some of the profit tends to leave the area, though as many of Vejer's businesses are owner-run, this tendency is not as marked as it is elsewhere. Too much tourism, as the nearby Costa del Sol shows, can extinguish a town's identity and remove its dignity. Changes must be thoughtful and well-researched and the tourist industry, however powerful its lobby, should not be allowed to interfere with the traditional life of the town.

As I write, in the middle of 2014, the developed world is in the process of emerging from a recession, described locally as the 'crisis'. Local industry has risen to the occasion, producing 'crisis bread' and other products. Unemployment nationally stands at around 20%; in the Province of Cádiz, it is over 30%. Despite Andalucía's rich agricultural resources, the service centre dominates the economy. A property building boom collapsed when the crisis hit. As in the past, work is seasonal and short term and increasingly hard to get. The nineteenth century is closer than we think.

What became of the lush grasslands of Andalucía, the streams, pastures and orchards envied by the Romans, the Goths and the Moors? In a sense, they are still with us. Andalucía is the least industrialized area in Spain; its sheep and cattle roam at large, half the territory is still covered by trees. Half Spain's metal is mined in Andalucía. Vejeriegos still produce honey on the surrounding hills.

Whatever steps are taken to revitalize this beautiful and fertile part of the world, care for the environment must be a major consideration. At present, Andalucía only produces 7% of its domestic energy through renewable energy sources, compared to 70% in Galicía, with a similar terrain. This can be improved on, and should be, despite the protests of some incomers.

The history of Vejer has been a patchwork of events, harsh and terrible, mundane, inspiring and brilliant. Through the centuries, the town has fallen and risen again time after time. It stands before us now, more bewitching than ever before. It will survive.

Vejer de la Frontera—A History

To discard, however, everything wild and marvellous in this portion of Spanish history is to discard some of its most beautiful, instructive and national features. It is to judge Spain by the standard of probability suited to tamer and more prosaic countries. Spain is virtually a land of poetry and romance, where every day life partakes of adventure, and where the least agitation or excitement carries every thing up into extravagant enterprise and daring exploit.

Washington Irving, Legends of the Conquest of Spain

PART TWO

LEGENDS

Vejer has a strong oral tradition, which has not suffered through the advance of literacy or the influx of visitors. Many of these stories were originally written down by Antonio Morillo Crespo and published in Boletín, the journal of the Society of Friends.

Habas

At the beginning, the forests of Tartessos were inhabited by the Cunetes, whose king, Gargoris, first discovered how to collect honey. When his daughter had an illegitimate son, whom she named Habas, Gargoris decided to kill him to escape shame. He exposed the child on the hillside, but when he sent someone to collect the body, the baby was found to be alive, having been fed by animals. Some time later, Gargoris deliberately placed the child in front of a herd of cattle, with the intention of submitting him to a slow and terrifying death, but once again the child survived. Gargoris tried again, locking him away with some starving dogs, but the dogs protected Habas. Infuriated, Gargoris threw the boy into the sea, but he floated back to shore, where a deer carried him away to run with the herd. For years, Habas lived with the deer, but one day, he was caught in a trap and brought before the king.

Gargoris recognized Habas by the many scars he had given him as a child, and was amazed that he had survived. He decided that Habas was under the special protection of the gods and named him heir to the throne. When Habas became King, he made many changes. Having eaten wild food in the forest, he encouraged his people to follow a civilized diet. He also organized the labour force into seven different classes. After he died, his descendants ruled for many generations.
Justin, (2-3rd centuries AD) Epitome 44.4

The Legend of Roderick and Florinda

After taking power in Toledo, King Roderick began to receive visits from the noble families of Spain, including the deposed Witiza's brother-in-law, Count Julian, the lord of Algeciras, who had successfully held back a threatened Moorish invasion. To assuage Roderick's doubts, Julian left his daughter Florinda to be raised at court. One afternoon, Roderick caught sight of the naked Florinda and was consumed with lust. Although Florinda resisted every blandishment, Rodrigo finally 'triumphed over her weakness by base and unmanly violence'. The traumatized Florinda wrote at once to her father, begging to return home. When the news of Florinda's rape arrived, Julian vowed revenge. Riding to Toledo, he reported that the danger of Arab invasion had passed, and advised Roderick to send his army north, leaving southern Spain undefended.

Julian returned Florinda to her mother, and they plotted to depose Roderick and restore the line of Witiza, whose sons were in exile in North Africa. He then visited the Arab General Musa, promising to deliver Spain into the general's hands. Twelve thousand men were assembled, and they sailed to the rock Calpe, from where they defeated the 'hardy, prompt and sagacious' Christian noble, Theodemir. Calpe was renamed Gibel Tariq – Gibraltar - in celebration. The defeated Theodemir sent to Roderick for reinforcements, but Roderick did not respond and the invaders swarmed into Spain, reinforced by Julian's cavalry. When he finally arrived on the battlefield, Roderick was dismayed to see Julian's troops encamped alongside the Moors. His inexperienced troops fought bravely through the morning, but when a troop of renegade Christian cavalry arrived, the Visigothic army fell, delivering Andalucía and Spain itself into the hands of the Islamic invaders.
Washington Irving: Legends of the Conquest of Spain

The Legend of Hicham and María

According to oral history, the castle of Vejer dates back to the Romans and Phoenicians. As there was no water supply within the walls, the castle was unable to resist a lengthy siege, so a passage was built between the castle and the biggest cave of la Barca, immediately beside the river. The passage remained undiscovered, and the occupants of the castle were unaware of it as the entrance, on the Patio de Armas was carefully concealed. Only the governor and his trusted servants knew it was there.

In 1264, after the Moors were conquered, Muslim guerilla Hicham Ibn Amar still lurked in the mountains. At the foot of the hill on which Vejer stood, in *el Concejo de la Villa,* lived a horse breeder called Rodrigo, with his wife and his daughter, María. The new Christian administration needed horses, and so the Castle governor told Rodrigo the secret of the passage, and the next time bandits approached, Rodrigo took his family up to the castle.

Shortly afterwards, Hicham Ibn Amar arrived in Vejer. One evening he met María and the young couple fell in love. María agreed to join the Muslim rebels. After searching unsuccessfully for their daughter, Rodrigo and his wife decided that she had been abducted by Moorish brigands, and they took their complaint to the governor. A tribune was called and the judge agreed that if María wished to return to her parents, she should be allowed to do so.

María preferred to stay with her new husband, and bid her parents a tearful farewell. But if María ever told her husband about the secret passage, he did not take advantage of the information, and in the years that followed Vejer survived both siege and enemy attack.

The Destruction of Patria

According to the story, a hundred Moorish knights lived in Patría, brave and skilled in war. Mounted on white horses, they used to ride out and devastate the area. On one occasion, having been informed that the knights were planning to attack Christian territory, the people of Jerez decided that they would have to capture the Moorish stronghold. Under cover of the night, they draped their horses with white sheets, and rode up to the walls of the enclosure, pretending to be the Moorish knights returning, loaded with booty. The people inside, unaware of the deception, opened the doors and were captured. While some of the Jerez people remained behind to guard the stronghold and its captives, the others lay in ambush at the top of the hill, waiting for the Moorish knights. When they arrived, they were taken by surprise, and though some were surrounded, others escaped. The people of Jerez ransacked the villa, confiscated the cattle and enslaved the remaining Moors. The chronicler added that at the time of writing, some of the foundations and other parts of the building were still visible. Since then, its stones have been re-used in many buildings by the residents of Vejer and the surrounding area.

The Corredera Millstone

There are two millstones at the end of the Corredera, where the balustrade begins. The stones were both used for pressing olives to make olive oil. One, the newest, is conical in shape. The other, a round stone, is much older, maybe a thousand years old, and this stone has a romantic history.

After the Reconquista, most of the Moorish occupants of Vejer went to live in Granada or Morocco, but Ahmed the miller decided that he would prefer to stay. His mill, at the bottom of the hill near the river Barbate, was operated by a donkey which turned the mill wheel.

Ahmed was popular with all his customers, but he was also very handsome, with many female admirers. In the evening after he finished work, he would plunge naked into the river to cool off, and local girls would linger over the family wash in the hope of catching sight of him.

One day, a young Vejeriega woman spent the day with Ahmed and helped him to guide the donkey and turn his mill. The fresh air, and the smell of the ripe olives, combined with the circular motion, put her into a kind of swoon. She went home at the end of the day, but shortly afterwards, she disappeared and was never seen again.

After a while, the fuss died down, but a year or so later, another young girl disappeared under similar circumstances. Yet again, the girl disappeared without leaving any sign and was never found. As time went by, rumours came to Vejer of similar disappearances in the nearby villages.

One evening, a customer decided to follow Ahmed home after his work at the mill. He noticed that the young man disappeared into a space in the trees, and when he went that way himself, he found a high wall with trees growing around it. Looking through the gate, he saw a beautiful house surrounded by fragrant plants. Music flowed out through the windows. As he watched, the man saw Ahmed coming out of the house with a pretty girl on either arm, and following behind, both the missing girls from Vejer, with six or seven others. He realized that he had discovered Ahmed's harem.

The man decided that he should go back to town and fetch some men to break into the house and bring the women home, so he went back to Vejer as fast as his legs could carry him. He returned an hour later with all the men in town behind him, but however hard they looked, they never found Ahmed's house, or even one of the girls who lived there.

The Ghosts in the Church

Padre Manuel was a priest in Vejer. He carried out his duties diligently, but he disliked taking confession, which he found disturbing. One day, he heard an unusually sweet and serene voice from the other side of the screen, a girl, speaking with the freshness of youth. He was deeply affected by the meeting and found that he could not help looking for the young woman during services; however, since most women veiled themselves during church services, he was unable to recognize her. He tried to suppress his feelings by prayer and good works, but he thought constantly of the young woman in the confessional. One day, though, he saw her, and fell back, pink and confused into the confession box. She made her confession and he was enchanted, absolving her almost without listening to her words.

He continued to hear her confession for months, until one day he heard that she was gravely ill with consumption. Her grieving parents told him that she wanted to make her last confession. Padre Manuel could hardly bear his misery. His legs were weak and he trembled. He wept through her last confession and finally stumbled out into the street, heartbroken.

Years passed, and the young priest grew older. One day, alone in the church, he saw a woman's shape passing behind one of the pillars. He sat silent, without moving, and when she raised her veil beside the altar, it seemed as though the rose window behind her broke into a thousand lights. After that, he saw her many times, at Easter and other festivals, and he became obsessed with her spirit. One day, he died in the confession box, for no reason that anyone could see, and was found smiling softly, leaning over the partition. They buried him under the altar.

More than thirty years ago, while plasterers were working on the church, the wall which united the old and new parts of the church was removed. Some coins were found from the reign of Philip IV and an old parchment telling part of the story of Father Manuel. The rest was indecipherable.

The Babies in the Lake

The aljibes under the church, a thousand years old, would be of great interest to visitors and students alike, and on many occasions, the town council has been asked to open them to the public. The answer has always been in the negative, on account of the high cost of restoring them and making them safe. But beneath this lies a deeper and more sinister story. The council cannot open the aljibes, because as well as being an archaeological curiosity, they also are a graveyard for the unwanted babies of the conceptionista nuns, who would routinely drown their illicit offspring there without ceremony or remorse. The aljibes, therefore, are said to be littered with tiny skeletons.

Unpicking this story is complicated, because several historical realities went into its making. It is true that the town cemetery stood beside the church until the late eighteenth century, when it was declared full, and burial services were transferred to San Miguel. Unbaptised children could not be buried in the churchyard, but parents sometimes buried their stillborn children illegally, under cover of darkness, which might account for the presence of tiny skeletons in the area.

When excavations were made in the late twentieth century, some children's skeletons were found within the walls of the convent, but this is not proof that they were killed deliberately, or that they were the nuns' babies. It is just as likely that they were foundlings, who died of natural causes and could not be buried in the churchyard. It is very unlikely that the nuns would have polluted a water source by throwing dead bodies into it, and in any case, they had their own aljibe.

The City of Wicked Deeds (La Ciudad de Maldades)

This nickname is sometimes given to Vejer by its vecinos and others. It may refer to evil practices carried out during the Inquisition, or simply reflect a perceived general immorality on the part of its inhabitants.

The Legend of the Spirits on the Beach

Mariano, lived in los Caños de Meca, where he kept a small farm and lived close to nature. One day, he looked out sea, and to his astonishment, he saw two great navies engaging in battle on the sea before his farm. He climbed a tree to get a better view and watched as the ships fought. He had no idea what to do about what he had seen, and so he returned to his shack. The next day, he went out to look again. The ships had disappeared, but the tide had washed up dozens of corpses, some terribly wounded. Mariano decided that the bodies should be buried, and so he made a grave in the sand for each one of them, and said a prayer over each body. At the end of the day, he went to bed, exhausted, but pleased with his work.

Mariano waited for officials to come and ask him about what he had seen and done, but nobody else saw the battle, and not a word was ever said about the dead men on the beach .Some years after the incident, Mariano himself died, and his body was also buried in the sand.

The Legend of the Black Hand

In the 1870s, anarchists Arístides Rey and Elie Reclus arrived in Barcelona from France to introduce their ideas to the working people of Spain. They made their way to Andalucía, leaving their associates to spread the word in Madrid, where they soon formed an anarchist group, the AIT, which was later responsible for uprisings in different parts of Spain.

In Andalucía, legions of workers, disinherited from the earth they worked on, carrying with them an ancient grudge accumulated from one generation to the next, were fertile ground for radical ideas. The claim that the land belonged to those who worked it had a strong appeal to these underprivileged people. Before many years had passed, Andalucía represented 29000 members out of 50000 in the Spanish section of the Federation of Workers, making this region the pillar of international anarchism in Spain.

By 1878, Andalucía could no longer contain the revolutionary feeling of its people, and widespread rioting occurred. Cattle were killed, vines ripped out of the ground and farms were burned. In April, the riots in Jerez, which had reached the city, became a threat to national security as businesses were attacked and the houses of landowners were invaded. Similar uprisings took place in all the towns in the area.

The workers federation sanctioned these acts in a secret communiqué, telling its members to rise up against injustice and struggle for the Revolution. 'The workers would also like to eat', it pointed out, suggesting that the bosses were drones who deserved to die. When the authorities heard of this communiqué, they were scared, though not particularly ashamed. They began to exercise vigilance over country people, especially those with revolutionary leanings, and in 1879, a campaign began to suppress any kind of illicit association. They seized any papers they could find, and claimed to have accumulated information.

and done, but nobody else saw the battle, and not a word was ever said about the dead men on the beach .Some years after the incident, Mariano himself died, and his body was also buried in the sand.

The Legend of the Black Hand

In the 1870s, anarchists Arístides Rey and Elie Reclus arrived in Barcelona from France to introduce their ideas to the working people of Spain. They made their way to Andalucía, leaving their associates to spread the word in Madrid, where they soon formed an anarchist group, the AIT, which was later responsible for uprisings in different parts of Spain.

In Andalucía, legions of workers, disinherited from the earth they worked on, carrying with them an ancient grudge accumulated from one generation to the next, were fertile ground for radical ideas. The claim that the land belonged to those who worked it had a strong appeal to these underprivileged people. Before many years had passed, Andalucía represented 29000 members out of 50000 in the Spanish section of the Federation of Workers, making this region the pillar of international anarchism in Spain. By 1878, Andalucía could no longer contain the revolutionary feeling of its people, and widespread rioting occurred. Cattle were killed, vines ripped out of the ground and farms were burned. In April, the riots in Jerez, which had reached the city, became a threat to national security as businesses were attacked and the houses of landowners were invaded. Similar uprisings took place in all the towns in the area.

The workers federation sanctioned these acts in a secret communiqué, telling its members to rise up against injustice and struggle for the Revolution. 'The workers would also like to eat', it pointed out, suggesting that the bosses were drones who deserved to die. When the authorities heard of this communiqué, they were scared, though not particularly ashamed. They began to exercise vigilance over country people, especially those with revolutionary leanings, and in 1879, a campaign began to suppress any kind of illicit association. They seized any papers they could find, and claimed to have accumulated information.

Nothing changed, however, and the riots continued. Workers poached, picked berries from the hedgerows and demanded bread. In 1883, the hungry people of Andalucía were astonished when the Black Hand became national news, portrayed by the government as a semi-criminal organization, responsible for the mindless slaughter of women, children and helpless grandparents. According to Government reports, the Black Hand was the informal name given to a secret organization called 'the society of the poor against thieves and murderers: Jerez – Europe, 20th century'. The manifesto of the Black Hand apparently stated the principle of all-out war on the owners of capital, by any means possible. They were accused of plotting to bring down the government and put to the sword the ruling classes of the nation.

The bourgeoisie were subsequently provided with protection from the Civil Guard to put down peasant insurgencies and suppress the whole notion of change. Labourers were jammed into the already bulging jails and Blanco of Benaocaz, supposedly responsible for the 'Black Hand', was assassinated. On December the 4th, the evening before the execution, seventy members of a Junta supposedly swearing revenge on the ruling classes were arrested. In the following two weeks, the number grew to more than a hundred.

Not surprisingly, the riots escalated, and on June 4th 1884, 7 workers were executed in the Plaza del Mercado in Jerez. Many others were transported to colonies overseas. The organizers of the Black Hand, however, were never found, and to this day, Spanish anarchist groups deny, as they did throughout these unfortunate people´s trial, that the organization ever existed. It is now believed to have been a government invention created to give credibility to its suppression of workers' demands for justice at a time when class tensions were escalating throughout Spain.

The Legend of the Lake under the Church

One of the most pervasive ideas among expatriates in Vejer is the story that there is a underground lake beneath the Church. Various people claim that they know someone who knows someone who has seen it – the clear sign of what we now call an urban myth. According to the story, there are several boats on the shores of this lake, which is larger than the Plaza de España in some accounts. Somebody once told me that they had seen a photograph of the lake, and assured me that the boats were in place. I believe I have even seen this lake referred to on the Internet.

I would love there to be a lake under the Church – I even put it in one of my books. However, having raised the matter with local historians, including the authoritative Antonio Muñoz Rodriguéz, it is clear that it does not exist, or not in the form claimed by the story. The most likely source of the legend is the presence beneath the church of several aljibes, probably created during the Islamic occupation. Ángel Tinoco Chirino also points out that geological surveys reveal the presence of a body of water in the rock formation of the hill, probably a natural collection point for waters flowing down from the Sierra Nevada near Granada. However, this water has never been seen by human eyes, and certainly does not contain boats.

It was built quite in the beautiful taste of Andalusia, with a court paved
with small slabs of white and blue marble. In the middle of this court was a foun-
tain well supplied with the crystal lymph, the murmur of which, as it fell from its
slender pillar into an octangular basin, might be heard in every apartment.

Is not Spain the land of the arts; and is not Andalucía of all Spain that portion
which has produced the noblest monuments of artistic excellence and inspiration?

George Borrow – The Bible in Spain

PART THREE

CUSTOMS AND CULTURE

The Patios de Vecinos (shared patios)

'The patio is the wealth of the house.'

Although patios are common in Southern Europe and North Africa, and were used in the construction of Roman villas, they hold a special place in the culture of Andalucía. The patio is an environmentally effective means of dealing with hot climates, as it allows warm air to rise, while cooler air enters through openings at ground floor level. Well-placed plants and water features also help to lower the temperature. The narrow streets and white walls also found in warm countries similarly help to create shade and channel cooling breezes.

The shared patio, where several separate dwellings open onto the same space, is a typical feature of the province of Cádiz, and probably originated when larger homes were divided after the end of the seigniorial regime in the mid nineteenth century, though some shared patios reflect a local talent for inserting homes into tricky spaces. Vejer has around 250 shared patios in the old town. The typical patio is two or three floors high, built around a central area, but these are not always square, and some patios have a very idiosyncratic shape. Most are examples of local vernacular architecture, but a few, like the Casa del Mayorazgo, began life as grand houses, built for wealthy members of the aristocracy.

'Peeling potatoes in the Casa del Mayoazgo patio, 1950s

The shared patios represent the utmost of architectural ingenuity. They are designed to accommodate different ground levels, sometimes with entrances on two streets at two different levels. Entrances may lead upwards, downwards or straight ahead. It's sometimes hard to work out which patio is which because they are identified by numbers not names, and they crowd against each other, with one extending over the top of another in a pattern of inextricable complexity. Many have been carved into the rock face, many use materials The shared patios represent the utmost of architectural ingenuity. They are designed to accommodate different ground levels, sometimes with entrances on two streets at two different levels. Entrances may lead upwards, downwards or straight ahead. It's sometimes hard to work out which patio is which because they are identified by numbers not names, and they crowd against each other, with one extending over the top of another in a pattern of inextricable complexity. Many have been carved into the rock face, many use materials salvaged from an earlier period. Everywhere there are ravishing arches, stairways and window openings which speak seductively of the past, even the remote past.

Most houses consisted of a living/dining room and a bedroom or two, but before the present era, many household functions were performed in the patio. Most still have a communal 'retrete' in the entrance area, though these are generally disused. These communal toilets came in all shapes and sizes, with or without walls, doors or seats. People used zinc baths, first warming up the water in the communal boiler room, or over their own fires. Individual toilets in patio dwellings became the norm in the 1970s. Nowadays, most houses have their own bathroom, though there are still a few where occupants have to cross the patio to take a shower.

The bigger patios had boiler houses, usually near the stables, where water was heated for washing and laundry, and some of these are still in service. Many houses did not have kitchens, and cooking and washing up were also done in the patio, in specially built ovens either shared by several households, or for the exclusive use of one family. Where kitchens existed, they tended to be crammed into the most confined of spaces, sometimes barely large enough to stand up in. Woman often spent most of their days in these places, tending the fire and making meals. Under those circumstances, communal facilities would be preferable, even if you had to negotiate to use them. Later, when individual kitchens and bathrooms were built, they sometimes reduced the size of the patio.

Many patios contained stables, a necessity when a burro was the family car. The stables were often communal. Horses, donkeys and mules used the same entrance as people, except in very grand houses, so they are stoutly paved, sometimes using flagstones, though humbler patios sometimes had bare earth floors. The beautifully kept flagstone floors of many patios are a tribute to the hard work of generations of women who laboured to keep them clean.

Vejer's patios were inhabited by landless labourers, small house owners and tenants. A significant minority of residents spent part of their time in the country, where they worked and owned a small dwelling. They would return to the town for festivals or practical activities like visiting the doctor. The practice continues today, as many Vejeriegos also own country or beach houses.

Living in the close proximity of the patios, considerable skills of negotiation were required, though patios were often shared by different branches of the same family. Traditions and rules had to be observed, and these were passed on from generation to generation. The patio was the women´s province, as men often spent little time at home, passing their evenings in bars or clubs and very few Andalucían women worked in the fields, or anywhere outside the home.

Children were the life of the patio and often played in the entranceways. They were a major cause of patio disputes as they sometimes caused damage and were told off by whoever was passing, to the annoyance of their parents. The patio was the site of most celebrations, including wedding receptions and baptism parties, and would sometimes do service as an impromptu marketplace when fruit or vegetables were there to be sold. Funeral services were conducted on the patio, and there were always courting couples on the stairways.

Patios were functional places, and less space than now was devoted growing flowers and plants. They were crowded (at one time a hundred people lived in the House of the Widows) and there were often long queues to use the toilet. Doors, both outer and inner, were left open all day and only closed when darkness fell. Home life extended into the patio and most people were related in some way. When strangers arrived, caution was exercised.

In 1992, the Ayuntimiento initiated a yearly competition for the best patio, which takes place in May. Many patios are open to the public during the week of the event.

Aljibes

Until running water was introduced in all houses, drinking water was purchased and delivered to the patio or brought up from the wells at La Barca, but to water animals and flowers, clean floors, wash clothes or flush the toilet, aljibes provided water on the spot. *'Aljibe'* is the hispano-Arabic name for an underground rainwater collection cistern, a labour saving and environmentally friendly household item. The name derives from the Arabic *'al gubb'*. Aljibes were used to store the water which drained off the roof, and Vejeriegos distinguish between this and a pozo, which accesses underground sources. Most patios had at least one aljibe, normally constructed with brick floors and walls plastered in sand or lime.

The rain was collected by an ingenious array of pipes, gutters and channels, which directed the flow of water from the roof to the aljibe, often as large as the patio itself. Access points to aljibes sometimes resembled wells, but they came in a variety of shapes and sizes: closed, open, openings in walls, square, round, semi-circular.and in almost every part of the patio. In larger houses, aljibes and pozos were sometimes accessed from inside the house. There is a system of aljibes under the church, probably dating from the Islamic occupation. The aljibe which once served the Convento San Francisco can be seen at the churros bar on the Plaza San Francisco, where a glass floor has been installed.

Carnival

Carnival is an ancient tradition which probably goes back to Roman Saturnalia celebrations or even further. Later, it became incorporated into the Christian calendar, marking the renunciation of meat and other luxuries before the six-week fast of Lent (some interpretations claim Carne vale 'goodbye to meat' as the origin of the name). The oldest recorded carnivals took place in medieval Italy and the custom was gradually adopted by other Southern European countries. Later, the tradition moved to the New World. The main elements of Carnival are music and disguise, with processions and performances in various parts of town.

Carnival in Cádiz Province has a particular character, with a strong emphasis on social satire, and the musical forms used are unique. Groups of singers called *chirigotas* and *comparsas* perform in four different styles: The *Presentación* announces the group and introduces the theme. It can take any form or may even be spoken. *Cuples* are satirical songs with a chorus, relating to the theme and character of the group. A *Pasodoble* is a longer song without a chorus and usually with a serious theme. A *Tangillo* is a poetic composition, usually performed with an orchestra and the *Popurri* puts new words to current hits or other well-known tunes. The songs are never repeated in subsequent years, and it takes the composer around six months to put together the year's programme. Despite a decline in interest at the end of the last century, Vejer now has eight carnaval groups, six male and two female.

Vejeriego José Ruiz currently creates the town's Carnival repertoire, choosing a historical or cultural theme related to Vejer; in 2011, the topic was Juan Relinque. Local historians are consulted and the extravagant Carnival costumes are made locally. The *chirigitos* perform at various venues during Carnival, and there is a competition at the San Francisco Theatre. The Carnival costs around six thousand Euros every year, provided by sponsors and the local council.

The emphasis of Vejer's Carnival is satire and political protest, and writers and performers are often unpopular with the authorities. '*Viva la revolución!*' cry the people of Vejer in the *Popurrit*, Los Pleitos de Juan Relinque, while other songs castigate the Council for mismanagement or reflect on the fate of Osama Bin Laden's son.

People of all ages participate in Carnival, having as much fun as they possibly can and getting rid of all their wickedness in time for the serious season of Lent.

The Hazas de Suerte

The Hazas de Suerte are a unique feature of Spanish culture, dating back to the Reconquista. As part of the redistribution of land in 1288, it was agreed that the council should in future share out all vacant lands, creating plots of different sizes according to the social status of the recipients. In 1307, Alfonzo Perez Gúzman was given jurisdiction over the town, and in consequence, the sharing out of the land passed into the hands of the Dukes of Medina Sidonia.

By the 16th century, these rights were not observed and illegal taxes were imposed, leading to Juan Relinque's protest of 1564. Several rules applied to the allocation of the hazas. Occupants were required to have 20 years continuous residence in Vejer and a yunta of oxen to qualify. Once qualified, the rule was 'first come, first served', creating an unseemly race to the hazas. Fearing for their dignity, aristocrats preferred to hire teams of athletic types to race down the hill and dash across the fields to stake their claim.

When the Crown tried to take back the hazas, for once Dukes and town were united in protest, and appealed successfully to the courts. In the nineteenth century, some of the hazas were signed away to the company draining the La Janda Lake. Other applicants had to be male, over 25 and own some property. In 1840, the town's wealthy residents tried to privatise the hazas, and were prevented from doing so by the crusading Mayor Diego de Luna. In 1864, the state tried to do the same thing. This time, they had the united forces of Eduardo Shelly, the Marqués de Franco and the Condé de Niebla to deal with, as well as the local council. They rapidly caved in and a celebratory bullfight was held.

At present, there are hazas in 13 locations, each measuring 150000 square metres, mainly used for growing cereals and other crops. Arrangements for allocating the hazas are regularly reviewed to meet changing circumstances, and the last adjustment was made in 2007, when the rights of the unmarried and their children were recognized and it was confirmed that holders of Hazas can also have other jobs. Names of the eligible are taken from a special list, called a Padrón, and the Hazas are allocated on December 22nd of every leap year, with bass drums emphasizing each allocation, and a special drum roll for each of ten senior citizens. The system is controlled by the Junta de Hazas de Suerte el Comun de los Vecinos, presided over by the Mayor.

La Cobijada

The *Cobijada*, the covered lady, has been adopted as one of Vejer's icons. Her costume, which originated in 18th century Castille, consists of the *manto* and *saya*, a practical combination which became a kind of national dress. The costume is traditionally black, a respectable colour for married women. The *manto* can be pulled provocatively over one eye, or allowed to fall over the skirt, leaving the arms free.

Several administrations attempted to ban the costume, but it was tolerated in country districts and survived into the twentieth century. In the troubled years leading up to the Civil War, the authorities made it illegal to wear the *manto* and *saya*, claiming that they might be used to conceal weapons and disguise malefactors. When the government tried to revive the tradition in the 1950s, most women had converted their coverings into modern garments, and very few examples were left intact. Nevertheless, a few older women did continue to use this mode of dress into the 1970s.

Vejeriegas. 1855

The *cobijada* coverings are not a burka as worn by some Muslim women, and do not date back to the Islamic occupation; Muslim culture was suppressed after the repopulation, but until the twentieth century, all women were expected to cover their heads in public. *Manto* and *saya* were regarded as family property and passed on from mother to daughter, which extended their lifespan. With their straight front panel and defined waist, they would have done nothing to conceal a pretty figure, and at a time when many women were thin, would have enhanced the impression of femininity. The garments were made of gabardine.

'La Cobijada' has become an icon, and can be seen at most local celebrations. During the Feria in August, Vejer now holds a yearly competition to appoint the Cobijada of the year, electing a junior and a senior version who go on to represent the town at official functions.

Flamenco

'Flamenco is to love and live, to understand and smile, at this and that and something which is beyond.' Manuel Machado.

Flamenco began in Western Andalucía, and Cádiz, Seville, Jerez and Huelva all claim to be its birthplace. It evolved over many centuries from a variety of souces, including Andalucían folklore and the descendants of Gipsy, Berber and Arab musical forms, emerging as a recognisable style at the end of the 18th century. Flamenco is associated with the Gipsy people of Andalucía, though much flamenco is also performed by payos (non-gypsies). Traditionally, flamencos are part-time performers, who follow other occupations during the day, and even those who achieve high standards may not be well-known outside their own circle. To perform effectively, a performer must develop the spirit of flamencura, a subtle and instinctive understanding of the form. Many descend from long-standing flamenco families.

Flamenco transcends the boundaries between high art, folk art and popular music and takes many forms, ranging from the folkloric Sevillanas through Flamenco Nuevo, and Flamenco-Jazz to Cante Jondo, the preserved tradition of the 19th century. Each performer creates an individual style, using elements from one or more of these traditions, possibly combined with elements from other musical styles.

Flamenco is based on a series of palos: songs and corresponding dances identified by consistent patterns of rhythm, harmony and emotion. It is musically distinct, often using the Phrygian mode, which is not used in other western European musical forms, and which can produce a unique, ambivalent mood.

Traditional flamenco performances are improvised from a shared repertoire; the principal performers are the cantaor/a (singer), tocaor/a (guitarist) and bailaor/a (dancer), though percussion may be supplied by a cajón, or box-drum. Palmas (clapping) and jaleos (calls from the audience) are formalized, and create a spirit of communion and unity between player and spectators. At its most profound level, flamenco can create a powerful emotional effect on performers and audiences, which is sometimes described as duende by intellectuals, though Andalucíans are more likely to use

Dancer Adrián Brenes at the peña flamenca Aguilar de Vejer

the term 'aire' to describe the state of ecstatic absorption which may occur during a flamenco session.

Most Andalucían towns have a flamenco club, or peña flamenca, where the art is nourished at grassroots level. The Vejer peña, "Aquilar de Vejer", is situated on Rosario, in the former church of the same name. During the summer months, it offers a varied programme of performance, as well as an annual cante competition for singers. Flamenco is also performed at different venues in the town during summer weekends. During the month of July, 'Flamenco from the balconies' is performed in various places around the town.

Flamenco is deeply engrained in Vejer society; there is a guitar school and several dance schools give displays in the San Francisco theatre and during the spring and August fairs. Through the winter months, *juergas* (flamenco parties) sometimes occur informally.

In November 2010, Flamenco was recognized by UNESCO as part of the intangible heritage of mankind.

Music in the Corners

During July and August every year, the Council organises a series of public concerts, usually on the area adjacent to Arco de la Segur, but occasionally in the Castle. Live music is often performed in, or outside, cafes and restaurants.

Markets

The reformed Mercado de Abastos on the Plaza San Francisco sells fruit and vegetables as well as drinks and tapas.
A Rastro (flea market) takes place on the first weekend of every month at 7 pm in the summer and 11 am in the winter.
In April, the Concentrate street market sells local art and presents poetry readings, flamenco performance and street theatre.
The Zoco Andalusi, a street market featuring Moroccan goods is held in July every year.

Events and Festivals

The following events and festivals are also held during the year:

Three Kings: On January 6th, a parade is held to celebrate the arrival of Caspar, Melchior and Balthasar. Around 8 pm, the kings throw gifts out of the windows of the Convento San Francisco on the Plazuela.

Semana Santa: the week before Easter is marked by music, floats and parades of hooded Nazarenos. The main parade occurs at around ten on Easter Thursday.

Toro Embolao: Vejer has revived the tradition of bull running, which takes place on the afternoon of Easter Sunday, accompanied by market stalls and street music.

Feria de Primavera: In April or May: casitas are erected on the Fair Field at San Miguel, and a flock of fairground attractions set up their pitch. There are displays of cattle and horsemanship, as well as Flamenco concerts. A little train runs from the Plaza de España to the fair field.

Corpus Christi is marked by a parade, and takes place on the second week after Whit Sunday.

Candela de San Juan: Celebrated on June 24th, this event marks the beginning of the summer solstice and is a fusion of the celebration of John the Baptist's birthday and ancient fire festivals. In Vejer, a collection of life-sized puppets convenes on the Plazuela in the evening, before being marched to the fair field at Buenavista and ceremonially burned. Later in the evening, the pyrotechnic Bull of Fire terrorizes and delights onlookers on the Plaza de España. Other celebrations include beach picnics and barbeques.

Velada de Agusto: On August 10th, Our Lady of the Olive is released from confinement at the Ermita de la Oliva, and, accompanied by a sizeable crowd, is walked up the Way of the Olives through the woods to the parish church at Vejer. The journey takes about four hours in the heat of the afternoon and should not be attempted without a hat and a supply of water. On the 24th, she is walked back again in the other direction for her long winter exile.

Feria de Agusto: two weeks in August are devoted to music, celebration and fairground attractions.

Navidad: at Christmas there are parades, featuring real animals, and the town echoes to the sound of devotional music. Many schools create a 'living crib' in which children create appropriate displays. In general, though, Christmas is a family time.

Candela de San Juan

How like a ruin overgrown
With flower's that hide the rents of time,
Stands now the Past that I have known,
Castles in Spain, not built of stone,
But of white summer clouds, and blown
Into this little mist of rhyme!

Henry Wadsworth Longfellow

PART FOUR

BUILDINGS, MONUMENTS AND PLACES OF INTEREST

Caves

The caves which once gave shelter to our primitive ancestors have not disappeared. La Cueva de Algar, east of Vejer, shows evidence of human occupation from prehistoric times and has clearly been excavated as a shelter. It consists of two parallel corridors 400 metres long intersected by shorter passages at right angles. For many years, it was used for the excavation of guano for fertilizer. At La Barca de Vejer, La Venta Pinto restaurant extends back into a substantial cavity, part of the extensive caves which once served the port of La Barca. These are now not accessible. In Vejer, buildings were commonly extended back into excavated areas. The Peneque café on the Plaza de España, extends into a cave which used to be a wine cellar, as does the Quatro Gatos restaurant on the Corredera. Other excavated spaces, complete with wall niches, are visible behind glazed doors on the Mayorazgo section of the old walls and at the foot of the Torre de Sancho on the Plaza de España, showing how these spaces were used for shelter and storage.

The Church

The Church of the Holy Saviour (el Divino Salvador), built on the site of an earlier mosque, is an architectural marriage of two different spaces – the Gothic Mudéjar building of the 14th century and the Gothic enlargement of the 16th/17th centuries. The floor plan, 18 metres by 21, is that of a conventional basilica with a rectangular apse. The ceiling vaults are of various designs, suggesting a prolonged period of construction. The Mudéjar style can best be seen in the larger chapel, where the ridges of the arched ceiling are decorated in an early sawtooth design typical of the period. In the nave are two pairs of Roman style columns crowned with capitals of Arab origin that probably belonged to the mosque which originally stood on the site. The bell tower also forms part of the Gothic-Mudéjar conjunction, and its construction must have originated with the minaret of the mosque. The higher parts and the capital were reconstructed after the earthquake of 1773.

The walls of the medieval church would have been painted with frescos showing biblical scenes. Two of these, both dating from the 15th century, have recently been restored, though they are much deteriorated. One, on a pillar near the main altar, represents St. George and the Dragon. The other, on the last pillar of the Evangelist nave, shows an unidentified saint watching over a sick man. On the altar of Las Animas (the souls) is a 15th century Crucifixion, a painted wood carving, also recently restored. Also possibly of medieval origin is the table of the High Altar, which is decorated with a pattern of wheels, or stars, a work of mathematical accuracy as well as beauty, which resembles the style perfected in Nazarin Granada. As mentioned earlier, the church was ransacked in 1936, but no structural damage was done.

The Church of our Lady of the Rosary

This deconsecrated church stands at the end of Calle Rosario. In the final days of its history, Mass was only said there on festival days, and in the days of the republic, the workers organizations requested that the church be closed and used as a people's centre. The parish refused this request. Having been damaged in the riots of July 1936, the images and other valuable property were removed (the Virgin of Pilar suffered 'various mutilations'). Two years after the riots, the church reopened with a makeshift altar, though it was rarely used. It was sold in the 1960s and is now devoted to Andalucía's other religion, flamenco.

The House of the Widows

This house, originally the home of the Naveda family, stands half way between the town centre and San Miguel. It has a beautifully designed and preserved arched patio. In 1890, Dolores Silva established a refuge here for poor widows. In the late nineteenth century, the house was home to more than a hundred people. The house was restored by the council in 1983, but still provides accommodation for homeless widows. The apartments are built around a rectangular patio with arches on three sides, and an open walkway on the first floor. The original access to the aljibe has been preserved as a feature.

The House of Widows is at Calle Juan de Sevilla 7, and can be reached by turning under an archway opposite Juan Relinque and following the road upwards.

La Casa del Mayorazgo

The house was built in the Baroque style at the start of the 18th century to house the administrators of the Dukes of Medina Sidonia's affairs in Vejer. A large and impressive property, it occupies an L-shaped site, the short arm of which extends to the Arch of Sancho. The façade was significantly altered in the twentieth century, when the protective ridges were removed from the windows and two new window openings were made on the first floor. The Baroque doorway, however, has survived.

The house is typical of larger Andalucían houses in having two separate patios, one being residential and the other devoted to stables and other services. As originally constructed, it contained numerous service areas, including two aljibes, a winery, a poultry yard, granaries, stables, a chicken run and a fixed washbasin for laundry. Unlike most, it also possessed a bastion and a tower with a bell gable. Most of the residential accommodation was situated on the first floor, and the area over the entrance was once a chapel, some of whose frescos have been preserved. The house in an excellent example of environmental architecture; shaded from the hot summer sun and cooled by large full-length windows, it was also equipped with heavy shutters which conserve heat by reducing the glazed areas during the winter.

When the seigniorial regime came to an end, the house was divided into nine dwellings, though this was later reduced to six. In the early

La Casa del Mayorazgo, 1926

twentieth century, fruit and vegetables were sold from the patio. The patios and tower are now open to the public.

The House of the Marqués de Tamarón

The Palace was built in the second decade of the eighteenth century for Bartholomew Juan Ahumada del Santisimo, Vicomte de las Torres Luzon. After the death in 1776 of Teresa de Ahumada, the last of the family, the building changed hands several times. In 1808, it was acquired by Arraf and Francisco Valdes, father of José de Mora, the Marques of Tamarón. When Arraf died, his wife inherited the house and carried out improvements and renovations. The Palace continued as a family residence until 1938, when it was sold to the local authority. Owing to the ancient outline of the surrounding buildings, the building has a trapezoidal floor plan which contrasts with the regular neoclassical façade.

For almost three decades, the building served as the headquarters of the local Civil Guard. After being acquired by the Ayuntimiento, between 1976 and 1980, it was used as a centre for professional development. The building was extensively restored by the Council in the early 1990s, and is now Vejer's Casa de la Cultura, housing the library and other administrative offices. On the ground floor, there is a preserved bread oven, and a permanent exhibition featuring different aspects of Vejer and the surrounding area, while the first floor houses regular exhibitions. The current Marqués, Santiago de Mora-Figueroa y Williams, is a writer and diplomat, who was appointed Spanish Ambassador to Great Britain in 1999.

The walls

The walled enclosure of Vejer represents an irregular polygon, with one wall each facing north, south and west, and two facing east. The walls are approximately two kilometers in diameter and enclose an area of some four hectares. They are between one and five metres thick.

Four gates gave access to the walled enclosure, which apart from the Puerta Cerrada, which, as its name suggests, was closed for centuries, correspond with ancient local roads – the Puerta de la Villa with the Cuesta de la Barca, and Fuente del Consejo, the Puerta de Sancho IV with the Cuesta de Cagajón and the Medina Sidonia road and the Puerta de Segur with the Cruz de Conil road to Cádiz. The most accessible entrance, la Puerta de Segur, was defended by asmall enclosure known as 'The Bulwark', corresponding with the round tower and the stretch of wall behind the Casa de Tamarón. This enclosure, which was built in the late 15th century under Enrique de Gúzman, second Duke of Medina Sidonia, originally had a strictly military function.

The construction of the walls generally consists of large, regularly shaped stones of various sizes, held together with mortar. However, the square towers and the Sancho and Segur gates are made of rectangular, carved stones of a regular size. The square tower on the Corredera, exceptionally, is an excellent example of stonework. The towers had vaulted chambers set into the battlements as can be seen in the Tower of the Mayorazgo. The ribbed vault with horns inside the Corredera tower is a Mudéjar feature characteristic of the 15th century.

The walls have been the subject of considerable restoration since 1976.

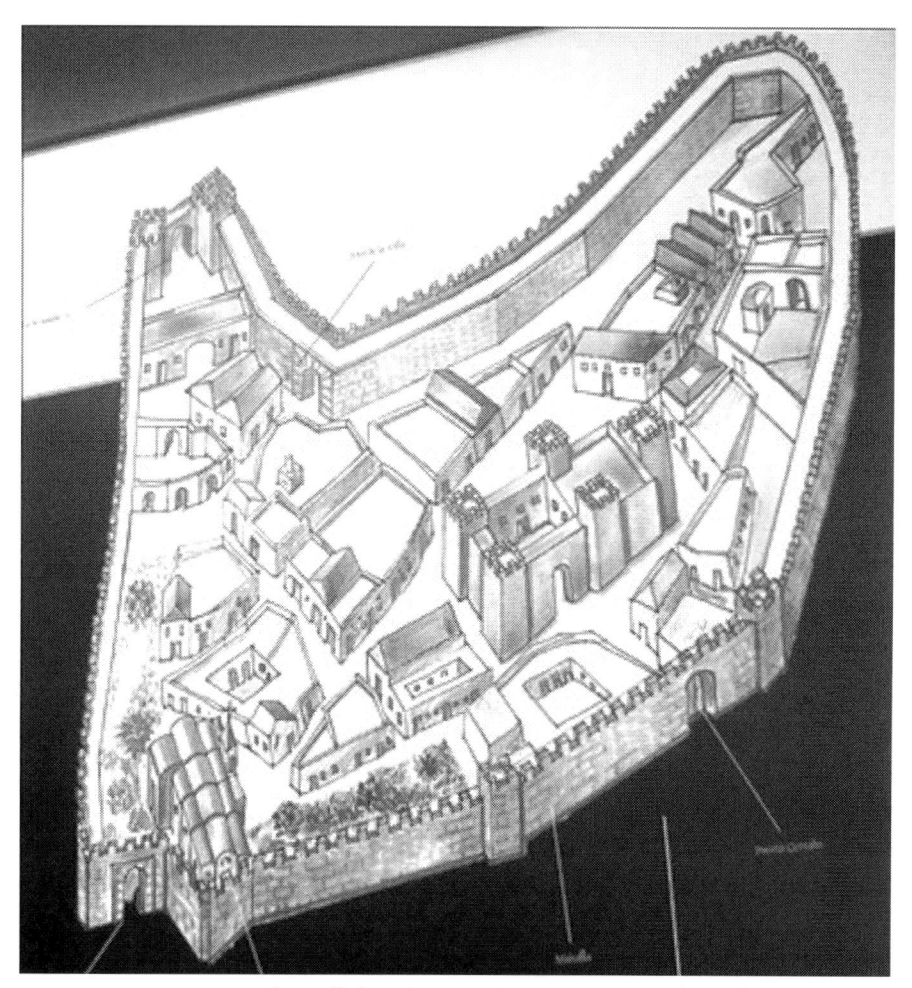

The Walled Enclosure . Biblioteca de Vejer

Excavations of the Church and the walls in 1987 and 1990 produced abundant quantities of Roman, Punic and Iberian pottery and part of the old foundations was dated to the late Bronze Age. In all probability, the current enclosure was commenced by the Moorish occupiers in the early Middle Ages; the Christian troops who liberated Vejer in the 13th century must have found the walls more or less as we see them today.

After the late 16th century, very few additions were made to the town's defences, and around 1750, the tower next to the Church of the Conception was demolished. At the start of the 19th century, in a attempt to improve the town, the first gate of the la Segur bulwark was taken down, the stretch of wall which linked the house of the Marques of Tamarón with the circular tower of the Parish Church was removed, and the stretch of wall between that tower and the Convento of the Conception was demolished.

Gate of Sancho IV

C/Corredera

This gate dates from the tenth and eleven centuries and was restored in 1973. It is made of quarried stone and a seigniorial escutcheon appears on the side facing the Corredera.

Mayorazgo Tower

Casa del Mayorazgo

This tower was built between the tenth and twelfth centuries. It is now part of the Casa del Mayorazgo, but was in existence for many centuries before the house was built. The tower was intended primarily as a lookout, with a commanding view of the maritime approaches. It has a small bell tower, which was used to alert the population of approaching pirates. The tower also has a small indoor chamber where the guard could warm themselves between watches. The tower is open to the public through the Mayorazgo patio.

The Arco de la Villa

Plaza de España

The Arco de la Villa was built in the tenth century. It was the least substantial of all the town arches and was altered many times over the years, until by the 1950s it was virtually derelict. It was rebuilt on a modern scale and widened. Above the arch, there is still a small room which was added in the 19th century.

The Arco de la Segur

C/Marqués de Tamarón

The most accessible of the town gates, this archway was first built in the tenth century. In the 15th century, a balustrade was added, flanked by two cylindrical towers. On the outside of the arch is a plaque bearing the coat of arms of the Mendoza family. The arch was restored between 1974 and 1978.

Puerta Cerrada

C/Mesón de Ánimas

Also called the Barbary gate, this gate was permanently closed for centuries. It was the most exposed of all the city gates and the most vulnerable to pirates, as it faced the coast. It did not correspond with any major roads, although when built, it would have provided immediate access to the Castle.

The Corredera Tower

C/Corredera 7 José Castrillón

A rectangular tower made of quarried stone; this was the last one to be built, and probably dates from the fifteenth century, at the same time as the alterations around the Puerta de la Segur. This tower rises above the level of the walls and was certainly used for surveillance purposes, with a grandstand view of the surrounding countryside. Evidence of fires found inside the tower suggest that it was also used as a signal point, with the purpose of alerting the neighbouring areas to possible attack. It was last restored in 1974.

The tower can be accessed through number 24 Calle José Castrillón, though it is usually necessary to phone for an appointment.

The Tower of San Juan

The Tower of San Juan

C/San Juan

This tower is on the same level as the wall. Its function was to watch over the coast, and it was provided with fixings to secure crossbows if an attack should occur. The tower has not been restored and so gives an interesting example of how Vejer's walls and towers looked prior to the 1970s. It is only accesible through a private house, but can be seen from Calle San Juan.

The Castle

C/Castillo

The Castle was a part of the system of fortifications in Cádiz, stretching from the estuary of the Guadalquivir to the castle at Tarifa. From its beginning to the present day, the Castle has been the site of numerous reforms, giving us a rich variety of different architectural styles, beginning in the 9th century with the Moorish double gate of the Islamic taifa and continuing to the final additions in the 18th century. The castle is constructed of irregular stonework, held together with lime mortar.

The Castle is situated at the highest point of Vejer, creating an important

The full extent of Vejer's castle is best seen from a distance.

landmark. One of its peculiarities is that until recently, part of it was used as a private residence, adding an ethnological dimension to its historical interest.

The castle has a floor area of 74 metres by 24, with towers on the northeast and northwest sides. It includes additions made to the southeast side and in the 15th century, additions were also made in the area of the access gate. The castle can be classified into two different areas, the military enclosure to the north west and the residential area, once the Vejer home of the Dukes of Medina Sidonia.. This is the area which has been the most modified over the years.

Two styles can be seen at the entrance, the 15th century outer gateway and the 11th century Muslim horseshoe arch. Initially, this was a simple entrance, but it was later remodeled to resemble the entrance to the Medina at Córdoba, with identical facades facing inward and outward. Very little remains of the Islamic era, except the alfiz with a flower motif, the dome over the space which links them, and the interior façade. The exterior Muslim façade was almost completely destroyed in the 15th century when the new façade was built.

The patio was the centre of the residential part of the Castle. It is L shaped, measuring around 140 square metres, and has three distinct parts. The first at the entrance, at a lower level, is paved with brick. This area provides access to various dependent buildings and the well. Steps lead up to the second patio area, giving access to the residential area. This part of the patio is surrounded by stonework benches, plastered and lime washed, and floored in slate. A passage in the left corner leads to the military enclosure. The ground floor rooms would have been used for utilities of different kinds, as well as accommodation for servants. Among the features accessible from the patio are a 15th century well and a stone oven which would have been used to heat a two storey separate dwelling which once existed within the Castle enclosure.

In the south corner, there are stables with two bays, parallel with the south west façade, There was a forge, and even the iron work feeding troughs and tethering rings are still visible, as well as a wood burning stove. A staircase at the side of the stables leads to an old granary on the upper floor, which was used as residential accommodation in the 20th century.

The first floor walkway, added in the 18th or 19th century to provide separate access to the different rooms leads to the living accommodation. Until the end of the 19th century, the living accommodation was confined to the sides with the portico, except for the kitchen which was on the south east side, but at the beginning of the 20th century, the space was divided into separate dwellings and the old granaries were connected with the area that looks onto the military enclosure. The rooms in the north east and north west overlooking the military enclosure were probably formal apartments.

The Castle was declared a National Monument in June 1931, and in April 1949, was placed under the protection of the state as a military relic. In June 1985, it was declared a site of national interest under the national heritage law of the same year. It is currently in the hands of three separate owners, with plans to bring the whole building under the jurisdiction of the Council in the near future.

In 2012, the stables were redisgned as a museum of everyday life in the 1940s to 60s, which is open to the public when the Castle itself is open.

The Convent of the Conceptionistas

Calle del Castillo

The Convent was financed by Vejer nobleman Juan de Amaya el Viejo and his wife as a burial place, and completed in 1584, by which time they had both died, and been buried elsewhere.

Initially it was occupied both by the nuns and by Franciscan monks, but the monks left within a few years and established their own convent on the site of the present Convento San Francisco. By 1618, the convent was already showing weaknesses, and these led to considerable damage in the earthquake of 1773. It was closed in 1835 after the Desmortisation, and subsequently sold.

In 1930, the Convento was in serious need of repair, and was purchased by the Castrillón family, who presented the building to the people of Vejer in 1996. A major programme of excavation and restoration ensued, during which many discoveries were made. The Convento is now used as an exhibition space.

The Convento of the Conceptionistas

Convento de la Merced

Plaza Padre Caro, C/Corredera

The Order of Mercy was established in Vejer in 1620 in some houses near the Santa Catalina Hermitage. The order proceeded to create this purpose-built convent which opened in 1646. The building was seriously damaged in the earthquake of 1773. Under the Desamortisation of 1835-36, it was abandoned and became derelict. In 1900, Padre Fernández Caro acquired the building and restored it, though he was not able to save the presbytery. The building is now the site of the junior section of El Colegio del Divino Salvador.

The Convento of San Francisco

La Plazuela

The Convento was built in the 18th century, on the site of an older building. Between 1835 and 1837, under the Desamortisation, the Convento passed into municipal use. The arson attack of 1842 caused serious damage, and an altarpiece by Juan de Oviedo was lost. At the end of the 19th century, the Enciso brothers purchased the building and used it as a commercial centre, adding three floors to the church building, which are still in use. The building was purchased and restored by the Ayuntimiento, who converted it into a hotel in 1988. The monastery church is now used as a cafeteria, where some 18th century frescoes have been preserved. The original chorus room on the first floor is used as a reading room, and the refectory is now a restaurant. The hotel also possesses a 2nd century Roman mosaic, which was discovered in Libreros.

The Convento and its associated cloisters, cells and the old sacristy, once spread over a considerable area surrounding the current building, including the Plaza San Francisco and La Calle del Cerro beyond it. When the restoration was carried out in 1979, several coins were found from the reigns of de Felipe IV y Carlos II, apparently intended to commemorate the laying of the building's first stone.

Since 1994, the hotel has been administered by TUGASA, the Cádiz tourist organization.

La Ermita de Nuestra Señora de la Oliva

Five kilometres from Vejer on the Barbate road

This site was first occupied by a Roman villa, which was later demolished to build a Visigothic Christian basilica, consecrated by Bishop Teodoracio in 674. The basilica was destroyed during the Muslim occupation, and rebuilt in the fifteenth century. Today's church, built in the Baroque style, was consecrated around 1770. Restoration was carried out in 2004. A Roman funerary inscription exists on the reverse side of a stone pillar which also records the consecration of 674. The Virgen de la Oliva spends her winters here before being escorted to Vejer for the Feria in August. Alongside the church, there are some monastic buildings, now used as retreats, grouped around a beautiful patio.

La Janda lake

La Janda, to the north east of Vejer was the largest lake in Spain, once reaching as far as Benalup. It consisted of a network of interconnected lakes, which joined during periods of heavy rainfall. Individual lakes were linked by shallow marshy areas, about 80 cms deep and thickly overgrown by water plants. The lake was drained between 1825 and 1967 and the reclaimed land was used for agriculture. The area of La Janda was the site of the Battle of La Janda, otherwise known as the Battle of Guadalete. La Janda was home to many birds, including cranes and marsh harriers. Today, the area is declared by Birdlife International to be Important Bird Area in Spain (IBA) No. 250. The basin is still visible from the Corredera when heavy rain floods the area.

The Ermita (chapel) at San Ambrosio

In the fourth century AD (so the story goes) Saint Ambrose and Saint Paul arrived in the area around Vejer (we are not sure which Saint Ambrose or which Saint Paul) and came upon a Roman villa which in its turn had been built on the site of some pre-Roman dwellings, which in their turn had been built upon some Tartessian houses...

The reason for all this building was the site – a gentle incline beside a small but reliable stream on the road to the coast. It seemed an ideal location for a new religious community, and in 644, some three hundred years after the visit of the saints, this aim was achieved. The basilica was built in the centre of the Roman villa, which the Goths seems to have taken over and used as workshops and accommodation. It was said to contain the relics of Saints Vincent, Felix and Julian, all martyrs. The church was consecrated by the Bishop Pimenio, who also consecrated churches in Medina Sidonia, Alcalá de los Gazules and Utrera. He was one of the most active of the Visigothic bishops, and played a major role in consolidating their presence in the area during the seventh century. He was also a friend of the saints Isidoro and Fructuoso.

Excavation of the site shows that it once included two pools, and had facilities for making wine, wax and honey, appropriately since Ambrose is the patron saint of bees. The chapel was repaired in the 15th century, but collapsed as a result of the earthquake of 1733. It has recently been restored to a certain extent and is now open to the public. The Ermita is not easy to find, as it is not marked from the road, but can be reached by bearing right on the road from Buenavista. After the sign marked 'Ermita', it is the second track on the left. The Ermita is reached by walking a short way up the slope and is signposted by the giant pieces of carved stone lying along the path.

The Roman kiln at los Navaros

The Roman kiln at los Navaros, as well as the remains of a Roman road, can be seen from the footpath the Ruta El Abejaruco (The route of the bee-eater). To find the start of the route, turn onto the A396 towards Medina Sidonia from the A48 (Cádiz-Algeciras). Take the first turning to the right, and follow the road which runs alongside the River Barbate to a car parking area on the left which marks the start of the route. The path is 4020 metres long.

Windmills

Vejer's windmills date from the mid nineteenth century, when the Dukes of Medina Sidonia lost their seigniorial privileges. The first examples were built in the Buenavista area. The purpose of the mills was to grind wheat, which had been previously been done by the water mills at Santa Lucia.

The first mills were not successful, and were replaced by more robust models. The windmills had rotating roofs which were moved to take advantage of wind direction, and four triangular sails. Windmills were later built in a more westerly location, and two of these now house restaurants.

The Aqueducts of Santa Lucía

The aqueducts are generally said to be Roman, further developed by the Muslims, but the theory has never been tested, and although the style and materials are similar to those used in Roman times, their use is unknown. There are several possibilities: the water may have been destined for Vejer, where sophisticated Roman water engineering could have pumped it to the top of the hill or it may have been intended for one of the salting factories near the coast. The system of creating artificial waterfalls to carry water downhill was used by the Romans in other places, notably Córdoba.

It has also been suggested the aqueducts are contemporaneous with the water mills they later came to operate, but if this were so, it would be reasonable to expect that they would be documented, as the mills are.

One of the Santa Lucía Aqueducts

However, no written record of their construction exists. The most likely explanation for their being found together is that the Dukes of Medina decided to exploit the aqueducts he found on the site when the mills were built in the sixteenth century.

There are two aqueducts, one at ground level, and one raised on arches. The first runs parallel to the road for at least 500 metres. The channel walls are of varying height, but in some areas are as deep as two metres; the water channel is roughly half a metre square. It seems very likely that this aqueduct flowed east to provide water for the Roman villa at Libreros, but more evidence is needed to confirm this.

The flour mills were first mentioned in 1561 when Pedro de Medina noted a river called the Algorrobo (carob) which drove six or seven watermills and irrigated most of the surrounding land. When Juan Relinque moved a plea against the Duke, he wrote 'in the said village there is a public fountain and the said Duke has placed there six or seven mills, while preventing others from constructing mills there.' In the 18th century, the Duke made 573 reales a year out of the surplus water from the mills. There is a footpath in Santa Lucia leading to the watermills.

La Barca de Vejer

Originally a ferry-crossing, La Barca was first mentioned in 1561 as a port from which numerous ships were sent with goods to Medina Sidonia. La Barca was a busy river port before Roman times, but it reached its height in the sixteenth and seventeenth centuries, when goods traded by the Dukes of Medina Sidonia went through the port. At this time, La Barca was an independent town, with around 700 residents and a church, St Nicholas. Trade declined during the nineteenth century and came to an end in the 1930s. There were two bridges at la Barca, and also two wells, from which most of Vejer's drinking water was drawn.

La Noria

A Noria is a mechanism for lifting water out of a well, normally for the purposes of irrigation. It was invented by the Arabs and arrived in Spain with the Islamic occupation. The mechanism at Buenavista was owned by a company in Barbate and operated for the benefit of the farmers and vecinos of Vejer. It was powered by donkeys, which turned a wheel to lift water into an aqueduct. Vejer's Noria, which went out of use around 1950, has been preserved, though the mechanism no longer exists.

'El creciente olvido de los nombres de cosas, de los oficios, de las plantas, de los lugares, no es más que una muestra de paulatino empobrecimiento de nuestro lenguaje, de nuestra historia, de nuestra cultura. Cada vez que se borra un nombre de la memoria colectiva es como si le condenaran a su desaparición la realidad y la historia que subyacen en esos objetos, esas plantas, esos parajes, esos oficios.'

(The growing tendency to forget the names of things, of trades, plants, places is just an example of the gradual impoverishment of our language, our history and our culture. Every time another name is erased from our collective memory, it is as though the reality and the history which resides in those objects, plants and trades were condemned to disappear.)

Antonio Muñoz Rodríguez. Boletín No 11.

PART FIVE

THE STREETS OF VEJER

Before the 19th century, the street names of Vejer were the result of popular consensus, and were not recorded by name plaques or street signs. Streets were named by their proximity to a building, a topographical feature, or the site of an industry or artisan area.

At the beginning of the 16th century, the suburb of San Juan was the first to be built., extending south from the Arco de la Villa. The town began to spread outside the walls and several new streets came into being, many named after different crafts and industries. New themes appeared in the 19th century when streets were named after public figures. These were frequently changed with the times; the Plaza de España, for example, has suffered nine name changes through the years. This list does not pretend to be exhaustive but does show some interesting connections. For many items in this section, I am indebted to Antonio Munoz Rodriguez´ series of 'Callajero' articles in the 1990s issues of Boletín.

Almizcate: A patio which runs between two properties giving both of them access to services like water and electricity.

Altozano: a hillock.

Arrieros: An area where muleteers lived and mules were kept.

Bodega de Triana: the site of a wine store: Triana is in Seville, and until 1880, the street was called Callexa Triana.

Callejón de Badillo was once Callejón de Arbolí, a corruption of Alfolí de la Sal, the Salt storehouse, where the public bought their supplies. However, Arbolí is also the name of a Vejer family.

Callejón del Escudero: Squire's lane .

Callejón Oscuro: dark alley, which it is.

Cerro: (the hill) was once called El Cerro del Bonete and led to the Virués winery established by Antonio Virués around 1750; he owned a small house and orchard on Los Remedios, which remained in the family until 1869. **Viña** also refers to this winery.

Cilla Vieja: named after the church offices which once stood there.

Corcheros: Site of cork treatment workshops.

Corredera: until recently, the Corredera began on Plaza Padre Caro with a steep slope. It was the town's main highway, much used by the Army, and for many years it was a male and aristocratic preserve. In 1875 a wall was built, and the roundabout appeared in 1900. In 1946, the houses on the north side were demolished and in the 1950s, the balustrade was built. In 1972, part of the balustrade collapsed and was rebuilt with slightly different columns in some places.

When the area was excavated to make the slope down to Padre Caro more gradual, the ancient foundations of the walls were revealed, and can be seen beside the Tower of Sancho. At different times in the past century, the Corredera was home to a telephone exchange, an open air cinema, the offices of the electricity company, a theatre and the health centre, as well as many shops. The street was once called Calle Diego Jose de Luna, after the popular Liberal politician.

Costanilla (de Don Eugenio): In July 1873, a Federal republic was proclaimed in Spain. Don Eugenio Pradier y Lima presided over the Committee of Public Health, a semi-revolutionary body which made many democratic changes during the course of the republic, including dismissing several corrupt public figures. When the monarch was restored, a number of street names were changed in recognition of Monarchist figures, but Don Eugenio was ignored. The people, however, did not need official approval to remember a man who had done so much to help them, and after his death in 1889, the street where he lived, La Costanilla, became known as La Costanilla de Don Eugenio. As he had no children, this is the only form in which his name survives.

La Cuesta de la Barca: The oldest and most direct route into Vejer rises from La Barca de Vejer, about 50 metres past La Venta Pinto restaurant in the direction of Barbate, where it is marked by an old steam roller. This route is not accessible to motor traffic, although it is paved. The path rises through a wooded area, emerging onto the Plaza de España via the Triperia steps. The road was in use in the middle ages, and local opinion generally holds it to be Roman, but it is probably much older.

Divino Salvador: The Parish Church.

Eduardo Shelly: a liberal deputy whose family originated in Valencia. This street used to be called Veracruz after the chapel which stood on the corner with Jose Castrillón Shelly.

La Fuente (the well): By 1834, the only available water in Vejer came from aljibes and pozos; the natural wells were at the bottom of the hill at la

Barca. There may have been an ancient well here, which did not survive the earthquake of 1773, or it may have been one of the routes down to the wells at the bottom of the hill. However, this street was previously called 'La Cárcel' after the prison there. During the nineteen fifties, the prison shared its site with a boys' school. Both were apparently run by a hairy-armed individual called Antonio Muñoz, who dispensed both correction and instruction with equal vigour. The prison building is now the Adult Education centre.

Gúzman el Bueno: Gúzman was responsible for holding back the Moors at the Siege of Tarifa; he was also the founder of the Ducal House of Medina Sidonia, the oldest dukedom in Spain, and the Ducal house which administered (and exploited) Vejer. **Juan Bueno:** The first Duke of Medina Sidonia; awarded by King John II of Castile in 1445.

Jesús: The name of this steep flight of steps is probably self-explanatory. There is no truth in the claim that it was named after the exclamations of those who finally managed to reach the top.

José Castrillón Shelly: several times the Mayor of Vejer in the late nineteenth century and a member of two of Vejer's wealthiest families.

Judería: the ancient Jewish quarter.

Juan Relinque: Once Calle Alta, this street was renamed after the sixteenth century activist who fought for the people's rights to the Hazas de Suerte. **Bellido:** Once Algarribillo (Carob tree), the street was renamed in 1950 to honour one of the judges who found in favour of Relinque.

Covarrubias: Originally La Laguna; renamed after another Relinque judge. **Rivas de Neira:** A third judge.

Manuel Torres/Yeseros: Plasterers' street. During the 18th century, like many streets outside the town walls, it was occupied by well-to-do artisans and farmers who gradually began to replace the old upper classes in political influence. In 1886, this street was renamed after

Manuel Torres was murdered in this house

Manuel Torres, the Liberal politician who was assassinated on this street in 1869, at number 8 (now 20).

Laneria: Site of a wool treatment workshop.

Los Remedios: named after a chapel which once stood close to the site of the present Information office on the way out of town. Part of the chapel is still standing and appears as an archway in the centre of the road. In the 1970s, when the restoration campaign was in full swing, the archway was part of a house, which was demolished to reveal the ancient stonework. The arch itself is blessed with a local nickname, which decency prevents me from revealing.

Misericordia is named after the Brotherhood of Mercy; it separates from San Juan at the point where the hospital used to be. The brotherhood disappeared with the desamortisation and the Hospital closed in 1890. In 1927, Primo de Rivero´s 'group of scholars' was accommodated here. The building has been restored and is now used by the Ayuntimiento.

Marques de Tamarón, of the Casa Tamarón, was the charismatic leader of a conservative family; this street was once Calle Panthéon, because it was adjacent to the church burial ground.

Mesón de Animas: an old name for an inn; probably at 1, Judería.

Merced: named after the convent and church next door –'Merced' signifies voluntary giving.

Molino Vizconde recalls the oil press in La Barca, which was owned by the Visconde de Torres Luzón, of an aristocratic Vejer family, in the middle of the 18th century.

Nuestra Señora de la Oliva celebrates Vejer's patroness, part holy virgin, part fertility goddess.

Palomina: this refers to the palomar, which collected the excrement of pigeons (palomina), for fertilizer.

Plaza de España: The Plaza de España took on its current form in the early 1950s when it was redesigned in the Sevillian Neomudéjar style, which became popular after the Universal Exhibition of 1929. The style is associated with the work of architect Anibal González and the ceramic tiles produced in the workshops of Triana, Seville.

The square, which originally lay just outside the town walls, probably existed as an east-facing cemetery during the Islamic occupation, and developed from this into an area for leisure and socializing. After the repopulation of Vejer following the Reconquista, the areas outside the walls, including the Plaza and the Corredera were used by the army and the nobility. By the end of the 15th century, the square had taken on its current appearance, surrounded by buildings which at that time were generally administrative, and was known as the Plaza de la Villa, or the Plaza Mayor. Among the most important buildings were the Casas del Cabildo, the Chapter houses, which were demolished in the 19th century to make way for the current Ayuntimiento.

Another important building was the Cilla, which dealt with Church finances. This was later known as the Juzgado and is now part of the Casa del Califa hotel. On the lower floor, which opens onto Calle Cilla Vieja, there were storage areas, while the upper floor contained the administrative offices. A Baroque doorway was added in the 17th century, and is now one of the Plaza`s most distinctive features.

Less refined, but equally important to the life of the town was the public slaughterhouse, which existed on the square for several centuries. It had an absolute monopoly on the meat that was produced and sold in the town. As the laboring classes in general could rarely afford to eat meat, it was mainly used by the wealthy, but its presence encouraged the development of a small market. The slaughterhouse was also the sponsor of bull running and other fiestas which took place on the square. Although these were the province of the upper classes, the poor were sometimes given meat as part of the festivities.

Until the beginning of the 18th century, the square, along with the Corredera, was the province of the upper classes, but it now became a much more democratic area. The main reason for this was a change in the conduct of the *Corrida*. Hitherto, it had been an equestrian activity, but with the decline of the nobility and the massive and costly slaughter of horses during the proceedings, the noble mounted toreador gave way to the plebeian matador, reliant on his own speed and skill and attracting audiences from all classes of society. The upper classes turned their energies to renting out their terraces and balconies for the enjoyment of *aficionados*. One of the most influential early matadors was Juan Conde, born in Vejer, who had his first experience with the bulls on the Plaza, and went on to become a *'maestro espadero'* and one of the great matadors of the 18th century.

As well as the corrida, the Plaza was the site of innumerable parades and other religious festivals. In the early 19th century, however, these were in danger of disappearing, as under French occupation, the town hall and the Convento de la Merced were seized and the square became the focus of social and political activity. From now on, all local protests and manifestations were likely to take place here, as well as public announcements. In 1837, the Square was renamed ´Plaza de la Constitutión.' Nevertheless, the *corridas* returned at regular intervals, whenever some local or national event was celebrated. The people of Vejer had a strong affection for the square as a venue for the *corrida*, and although two bullrings were built in the San Miguel area, they both failed to make a profit.

At the end of the 19th century, the *corrida* was banned from public places, and the Plaza was paved. It became a more sedate area for public recreation. A wrought iron palisade was built as a further adornment. During the terrible winter of 1912, when fields were deluged, country folk queued there for their daily allowance of half a kilo of bread a day, issued by the Ayuntimiento as a precaution against popular revolution. In 1931, the Republic was proclaimed by the united trades unions, and the square became the Plaza de la República for the second time. In 1936, the same square saw celebrations for the triumph of the Popular Front. Franco's regime, however, changed the name once again and the square became the Plaza de España.

The square continued to perform its function as a political arena, and the Church, serving as a symbol of the power and status of the nationalist-catholic regime, enjoyed a new prominence, using the square for a multitude of processions and other religious manifestations. In order to make space for these events, the square was denuded of trees and other adornments, and the prohibition of all other meetings and congregations left it empty and deserted until the present arrangement was created in 1953.

Poyete Soledad: According to Antonio Morillo Crespo, Soledad was a young woman who lived at the side of the Barranco de Almarez, which now divides the old and new towns. One day, her new husband left home and never returned. Soledad spent the rest of her days waiting for him, seated on the 'poyete' or stone bench at the corner of the street.

Retiro used to be Cantera after the quarry and its workers.

Reyes Católicos: this name was conferred on Fernando II of Aragón and Isabel I of Castille in a papal bull of 1496. The joint monarchs succeeded in defeating the Kingdom of Granada and financed Christopher Columbus' voyages of discovery to the Americas.

Rosario: after the former Church of the Rosary.

Sagasta: named after Práxedes Mariano Mateo Sagasta y Escolar, a Liberal politician who served as Prime Minister on eight occasions between 1870 and 1902. The street was popularly known as' la Hoya', meaning a dip, or hollow.

San Ambrosio: until comparatively recently, this street was the start of the road to San Ambrosio.

Sancho IV el Bravo was the Castilian king responsible for the repopulation of Vejer after the Reconquista. Sancho gained popularity in Vejer by creating the Hazas de Suerte.

San Filmo: San Firmo, a Christian martyr and the object of an early Vejeriego cult, though his existence is unproven.

San Juan originated with the foundation of the Hospital for the poor and the Church of San Juan around 1450 by Antón Pericón and his family. Both were highly valued by the community. Around 1500, the hospital and church were established as the Brotherhood of Mercy. This street encircles the walls, from the Plaza de España to the Puerta Cerrada.

Santiago: Saint James the moorslayer, traditionally the patron saint of Spain, though in 1817, the Cortés tried to replace him with St. Theresa. At number two, there is an ancient door lintol ornamented with a Living

Cross, a popular image in the fifteenth and sixteenth centuries. The street was built more recently, and this stone may have been rescued from a religious building after the earthquake of 1773.

Santisimo once marked the limits of the 17th century town. The name refers to the brotherhood of the Blessed Sacrament. The focus of Santisimo is Jesus Christ in the Eucharist and in the sacrament of his body and blood. The Confraternity of the Blessed Sacrament comes into its own on the Feast of Corpus Christi. When the road was being repaired in the 50s, a niche displaying the Santisimo symbol was found at no 11, suggesting that this was the site of a brotherhood meeting place or chapter. The devotion to Santisimo of the Ahumadas family, who lived on this street from the 16th to the 18th century, explains why the brotherhood met in that particular place.

Trafalgar commemorates the nearby Cape and the sea battle which occurred there in 1805. It was previously known as the Monte de Juno.

Tripería: A place where offal is processed, referring to the nearby slaughterhouse.

La Villa: Originally the residential part of town, reaching back from the Arco de la Villa.

Reyes Catolicos was originally named Cuartel Alto (high quarter).

Canalejas was Cuartel Bajo, (low quarter) but has had many other names in between. Part of **Callejones de la Villa** (lanes of the town) was renamed Sancho IV el Bravo in 1950.

Bibliography

Spanish:
Asaltos de piratas Berberiscos al litoral Gaditano de la Janda: Antonio Aragón Fernández
El Castillo de Vejer de la Frontera: Francisco José Cepero Sánchez: in Janda, Anuario de Estudios
Vejeriegos, November 2008
Rio Barbate: Diputacion Provincial de Cádiz 1997.Agencia Andaluza del Agua, Consejeriade Medio Ambiente, Junta de Andalucía (Ed)
Encuentros de Patrimonio, Historia y Costumbres 1997-2000: Ayuntimiento de Vejer de la Frontera
La ruta de los corsarios 2: Murcia y Andalucía: Ramiro Feijoo
Los Patios de Vecinos de Vejer de la Frontera: Jesús Melero Callado Manuel
Los Caños de Meca: Historia y Sueños: Antonio Morillo Crespo Vejer de la Frontera y su Comarca: Antonio Morillo Crespo
Los pueblos de la provincia de Cádiz 39, Vejer de la Frontera: Antonio Muñoz Rodríguez
Las Hazas de Suerte de Vejer de la Frontera: Ricardo Tejeiro
Memoria de Vejer Sociedad Vejeriega de Amigos del País
Boletín, 1-13: Sociedad Vejeriega de Amigos del País

English:
Clive Finlayson: Al-Andalus
Murray Sperber (ed): And I remember Spain
Bernhard and Ellen M. Whishaw: Arabic Spain: Sidelights on her History and Art
George Borrow: The Bible in Spain
Barry Cunliffe and John T Koch (eds): Celtic from the West: Alternative Perspectives from Archaeology, Genetics, Language and Literature
Joe Shwitter: Into the Blue
Hugh Thomas: Rivers of Gold: The rise of the Spanish Empire
Hugh Thomas: The Spanish Civil War
Mark Williams: The Story of Spain
Washington Irving: Tales of the Conquest of Spain

Diamond Eyes

Made in the USA
Charleston, SC
21 May 2015